Obstacles on the Path of Devotional Service

Obstacles on the Path of Devotional Service

Satsvarūpa dāsa Goswami

GN Press, Inc.

Persons interested in the subject matter of this book are invited to correspond with our secretary, c/o GN Press, Inc., PO Box 323, Mifflin, PA 17058.

Printed in India
ISBN 0-911233-80-6

First Edition: 200 copies
Second Printing: 200 copies
Third Printing: 1000 copies

GN Press gratefully acknowledges the BBT for the use of verses and purports from Śrīla Prabhupāda's books. All such verses and purports are © Bhaktivedanta Book Trust International, Inc.

Printed in India By Janta Book Depot (Printers & Publishers) New Delhi-110001.
For G. N. Press

Cover design by Madana-mohana dāsa

You mentioned that your pathway has become filled with stumbling blocks, but there are no stumbling blocks. I can kick out all those stumbling blocks immediately, provided you accept my guidance. With one stroke of my kick I can kick out all stumbling blocks.

—Letter by Śrīla Prabhupāda, December 9, 1972

Contents

Introduction

In a First Canto purport, Śrīla Prabhupāda states that there are many realistic obstacles on the path of devotional service, but by the grace of guru and Kṛṣṇa one can overcome them. What impressed me when I first read this was that Śrīla Prabhupāda and the Vedic sages are aware that we are faced with many problems when we try to take up the life of Kṛṣṇa consciousness. Sometimes we may think of sages as speaking in an idealistic way about complete renunciation of the world and the attainment of 100% pure devotion to the Lord. We wonder if they know what it is actually like for us to attempt this. It gave me solace to know that they *are* fully aware of our realistic problems. And we also must be aware of the problems, in order to solve them.

In the present age (Kali-yuga), the problems of life are worse than ever. As stated in *Śrīmad-Bhāgavatam*, "In this iron age of Kali men have but short lives. They are quarrelsome, lazy, misguided, unlucky, and above all, always disturbed." *(Bhāg.* 1.1.10) In his purport Śrīla Prabhupāda states, "The atmosphere is surcharged with opposition."

Of course, the obstacles in life are not created by the process of *bhakti-yoga*. *Bhakti-yoga* is meant to remove all problems, as stated in *Śrīmad-Bhāgavatam*: "The material miseries of the living entities, which are superfluous to him, can be directly mitigated by the linking process of devotional service." (*Bhāg*. 1.7.6) Sometimes it occurs to a neophyte devotee that his life was more orderly before he took to Kṛṣṇa consciousness, and so he thinks that devotional service is itself creating obstacles to his happiness.

The fact is that material life produces the problems. If Kṛṣṇa consciousness appears to make things worse, it is because we are stirring up the bad habits. If you leave your room dirty, it may seem undisturbed compared to when you sweep it and the dust rises, and everything gets moved around. But ultimately you are healthier and happier by cleaning.

One time a devotee wrote Śrīla Prabhupāda, "There are many obstacles on my path." Prabhupāda replied that he could remove all of those obstacles with one kick of his foot, but the real problem was that the disciple was not following the orders of the spiritual master. This statement gives us an indication of how the seemingly insurmountable problems can be resolved. As we study Śrīla Prabhupāda's instructions and share experiences of our struggles and successes, we can learn how to overcome the obstacles that realistically come to every devotional life.

In a general sense all the opposition we meet while performing devotional service is part of God's covering potency, called *māyā*. *Māyā* has two potencies: one is the throwing potency (*prakṣepātmikā*), and she also has a covering potency (*āvaraṇātmikā*). When the *jīva* initially misuses its free will, it is thrown into *māyā*. And even after we enter devotional service, *māyā* continues to test us. *Māyā* dictates, "Don't go to that Kṛṣṇa conscious temple." When we do go and engage in Kṛṣṇa consciousness, then *māyā* says, "Why don't you give up Kṛṣṇa consciousness? It's not making you happy." When we try to think of Kṛṣṇa, *māyā's* voice interferes. But for an advanced Kṛṣṇa conscious person, *māyā* is no longer an obstacle. Śrīla Prabhupāda writes:

> When a man becomes refreshed by association with devotees and awakens to Kṛṣṇa consciousness, he consults the activities of his mind—namely thinking, feeling and willing—and decides whether he should return to his material activities or stay steady in spiritual consciousness. . . . The mind may suggest that by *viṣaya-bhoga*, or sense enjoyment, one can become

> happy, but when one becomes advanced in Kṛṣṇa consciousness, he does not derive happiness from material activities.
>
> —*Bhāg*. 4.26.14, purport

In this little book I have not attempted a comprehensive study of every obstacle that comes to a devotee. I've selected problems that are of concern to most devotees and which I can relate to by my own struggles. I hope the treatment will have a positive effect as we think about these problems, read what Prabhupāda has said, and apply the remedies.

Philosophical Doubts

The *Vedas* teach that every living being is an eternal individual soul, and our constitutional nature is to blissfully serve the Supreme Personality of Godhead in the spiritual world. Since we are tiny souls, we have a tendency to misuse our free will, and when we do this we come into the material world, where Kṛṣṇa facilitates our desire to enjoy apart from Him. But this actually brings us continual suffering. As Prabhupāda says, "We are trying to exploit the resources of material nature, but actually we are becoming more and more entangled in her complexities." (SSR p. 165) Under the dictation of the material energy, we have to transmigrate life after life and experience manifold sufferings. If one is very fortunate, he meets a bona fide spiritual master and starts on the path of devotional service for going back to Godhead.

As we take to Kṛṣṇa consciousness, read Śrīla Prabhupāda's books and hear lectures by his devotees, we gain a theoretical understanding of this philosophy. It is a vast philosophy with many details. "One will find in the *Bhagavad-gītā* all that is contained in other scriptures, but the reader will also find things which are not to be found elsewhere." (Bg. 1.1, purport) Gradually our theoretical understanding turns into convictions and realizations. But even after years of practice, a devotee may again misuse his free will and revert to the rebellious attitude which brought the soul into the material world. Prabhupāda characterizes this rebellion as a duality of desire and hate. "Due to desire and hate, the ignorant person wants to become one with the Supreme Lord and envies Kṛṣṇa as the Supreme Personality of Godhead." (Bg. 7.27, purport) One form this rebellion takes is doubts towards the teachings of the revealed scriptures.

Let me give a practical example. While I was giving a seminar on *vandanam*, I explained my own practice of prayer. But I admitted that sometimes when I am praying to Kṛṣṇa a doubt arises as to whether Kṛṣṇa is really there and whether He hears me. I try to overcome this doubt by quoting to myself, "Ignorant and faithless persons who doubt the revealed scriptures do not attain God consciousness; they fall down. For the doubting soul there is happiness neither in this life nor the next." (Bg. 4.39) And sometimes I quote, "The doubts that have arisen in your heart out of ignorance should be slashed with the weapon of knowledge. Armed with yoga . . . stand and fight." (Bg. 4.42) Meditation on these verses has been helpful in curing my doubt.

One of the devotees attending the seminar said that he was a bit shocked to hear that a person who is supposed to be a spiritual guide could have doubts about Kṛṣṇa. I admitted to him again that unfortunately I am not above it. Until one reaches the liberated stage, doubts will continue to come. They may not be serious, or they can become so grave that they can seriously impede our progress. We should not hide the fact and bluff as if we are perfect. We have to learn how to deal with the obstacles on the path.

The Intellectual Approach

One response to skepticism is to fight back with knowledge. This is recommended by Kṛṣṇa in the *Bhagavad-gītā*, and we may refer to this response as the intellectual approach. Flush out that demoniac doubt and get it to speak to you. Enter into dialogue with your doubt. You can do this within your own mind or in a diary. Or it may be more helpful to talk with another devotee about it. Śrīla Prabhupāda used to encourage debate on his morning walks. He would ask the devotees for opposing views—"What do they say?"—and he would train us to argue against the atheistic points of view.

Let me raise a couple of doubts and respond briefly to them by the intellectual or debate approach:

1. "Kṛṣṇa consciousness seems to be just another of the many world religions and world mythologies that speak of gods and have a theory of creation and afterlife. So isn't the Vedic view a relative thing? And aren't all these religions really creations of humans?"

2. "Even if I accept that there is a divine force that is beyond the senses and the mind, how can I accept the exclusive viewpoint of the Vaiṣṇavas of India, that Śrī Kṛṣṇa is the Supreme Personality of Godhead? Does this mean all the other religions are wrong? I'm afraid if I follow Kṛṣṇa consciousness I'll just get into a narrow sectarian process."

A reply to doubt number one

You seem to equate all world religions with man-made mythologies. But the true science of God is beyond the creation of humankind and its poets. Do you think man is everything? Did humans create the sun and planets, do they create time and life and death? Can they control these forces? Not really, although puffed-up scientists may claim to. To begin to understand God and religion, you have to accept the existence of *acintya-śakti*, or inconceivable powers beyond human understanding. Since time immemorial, spiritually-minded persons have inquired into the existence of the Supreme, and God has revealed Himself to them in sacred texts or scriptures. Kṛṣṇa consciousness honors the truths found in other scriptures, but also teaches something more—a nonsectarian science by which all religions can be appreciated in their highest essence. That science is known as *Bhāgavata-dharma* or *bhakti-yoga*. *Bhāgavata-dharma* refers to the universal religion that is passed down by God to humanity, wherever it may occur in the world. Those who are sincerely interested in ultimate truths may consult this science by the proper method, and see for themselves. It is certainly unlike any ordinary book.

A reply to doubt number two:

The name Kṛṣṇa means "all attractive," and it is the all-inclusive name of God. Kṛṣṇa is revealed in the *Bhagavad-gītā* and *Śrīmad-Bhāgavatam* as the Supreme Personality of Godhead. Kṛṣṇa devotees do not decry the "divine force" as revealed in other religions. It is not a narrow, sectarian process as you fear. For example, the *Śrīmad-Bhāgavatam* describes the best devotee and the highest religion as follows: "The supreme occupation [dharma] for all humanity is that by which men can attain to loving devotional service unto the transcendent Lord. Such devotional service must be unmotivated and uninterrupted to completely satisfy the self." (*Bhāg*. 1.2.6) Does this definition of religion sound sectarian? It is not. It allows that *wherever pure devotion to the Supreme Lord appears in a total way, that is the best religion*.

You ought to inquire into the Vedic literature without a predisposition. If one is actually inquisitive, he is bound to gain spiritual insight from these texts.

Although these replies may be countered by the skeptic, we can counter-reply. As we go on preaching, we think of better arguments and we employ relevant śāstric references. In the case of the dialogue within us, the skeptic will usually be subdued by this method.

The method of dialogue is very satisfying because the arguments that Prabhupāda and the *ācāryas* give are competent. There is no reason to be overwhelmed by doubts when they come.

In order to confidently answer doubts, you need to study the philosophy. Within the Bhaktivedanta purports you will find constant dialogues. The opposing view is presented, and the Vaiṣṇava view is presented with reason as well as śāstric evidence. By learning this method of answering skeptics according to Vedic knowledge, you can deal with your own doubts; "over and above this, the reader will be able to convert others to accepting God as a concrete principle." (*Bhāg*., Preface)

To address doubts that are expressed in modern terminology, we can take help from learned Godbrothers like Sadaputa Prabhu, Ravīndra Svarūpa Prabhu and others who are trained in science and Western philosophy. When we hear from our Godbrothers, we will understand that their presentation is also based ultimately on the *śāstras*. *Ācāryas* such as Jīva Gosvāmī have given classical arguments as to why perfect knowledge cannot be gained by any person in this material world, because all conditioned souls are hampered by four defects: (1) The tendency to make mistakes; (2) illusion; (3) cheating; and (4) limited senses. Perfect knowledge has to come from beyond these human defects, in the form of *śabda-brahma*, revelation by Vedic knowledge.

In addition to studying, the "field work" of preaching will strengthen a devotee's convictions and arguments. Śrīla Prabhupāda writes, "All devotees, especially preachers, must know the philosophy of Kṛṣṇa consciousness so as not to be embarrassed and insulted when they preach." (*Bhāg*. 6.1.38, purport)

Faith Beyond Argument

Faith beyond argument does not negate the process of intellectual explanation or dialogue, but it admits that the absolute truth is ultimately beyond all logic. As stated in the scriptures, "Things that are inconceivable cannot be ascertained by logic." Logic should take us to the point of understanding that we have to go beyond human reasoning in order to know the source of everything and the nature of spiritual reality.

Faith is not only for simple-minded people who cannot think. Even those who argue against religious faith trust in the process of rational thought, or faith in the evidence of the senses or in scientific theories. We should never be embarrassed by the fact that we accept mysteries of higher knowledge on the basis of faith. Śrīla Prabhupāda always explained rationally *why* we should have faith in the perfect Vedic teachings rather than in imperfect speculation. Prabhupāda calls this "trust in something sublime." And so faith is very important in the discharge of devotional service.

> Those who are not faithful in this devotional service cannot attain Me, O conqueror of enemies. Therefore they return to the path of birth and death in this material world.

Purport

The faithless cannot accomplish this process of devotional service. Faith is created by association with devotees. Unfortunate people, even after hearing all the evidence of Vedic literature from great personalities, still have no faith in God. They are hesitant and cannot stay fixed in the devotional service of the Lord.

—Bg. 9.3

We should be confident in the process of hearing from Kṛṣṇa, and be satisfied to know that everything cannot be decided by intellectual debates.

Some Items of Faith

A powerful argument for faith that has always helped me is the existence of great spiritual teachers all over the world, at all times. Lord Kṛṣṇa, the Viṣṇu incarnations, Lord Buddha, and Jesus Christ all taught on behalf of the same mission.

> It is not a fact that the Lord appears only on Indian soil. He can manifest Himself anywhere and everywhere, and whenever He desires to appear. In each and every incarnation, He speaks as much about religion as can be understood by the particular people under the particular circumstances. But the mission is the same—to lead people to God consciousness and obedience to the principles of religion.
>
> —Bg. 4.7, purport

Aside from direct incarnations of God, many pure and learned representatives also give us cause for courage and faith. "One should have the common sense, " Prabhupāda writes, "to ask why, if Kṛṣṇa or Rāma were fictitious, stalwart scholars like Śrīdhara

Svāmī, Rūpa Gosvāmī, Sanātana Gosvāmī, Vīrarāghava, Vijayadhvaja, Vallabhācārya and many other recognized *ācāryas* would have spent so much time to write about Kṛṣṇa in notes and commentaries on *Śrīmad-Bhāgavatam*." (*Bhāg*. 10.2.35, purport)

We should have faith *and patience*. If we cannot understand something right away, we should wait until it becomes more clear to us. The philosophy is not proven defective just because we do not grasp it all at once. We will know when we are qualified.

Prayer is an important recourse for meeting every obstacle in Kṛṣṇa consciousness. So if a devotee has doubts about the philosophy, he can pray to Kṛṣṇa to please protect him. Prahlāda Mahārāja prays, "O my Lord [Nṛsiṁhadeva] please appear in our hearts and drive away our ignorance so that by Your mercy we may become fearless in the struggle for existence in this material world." (*Bhāg*. 5.18.8) By reciting śāstric prayers or by conversing honestly with Kṛṣṇa and Prabhupāda, we will become assured of their reality in our lives and the doubts will not plague us.

Another good response to doubts is to simply go on with regular performance of duties in Kṛṣṇa consciousness. We commit *acts* of faith whenever we perform Deity worship or chant Hare Kṛṣṇa. By performing these activities we trust in the process. This is called *śraddha*. Prabhupāda states, "In the *Caitanya-caritāmṛta* it is said that faith is the complete conviction that simply by serving the Supreme Lord, Śrī Kṛṣṇa, one can achieve all perfection." (Bg. 9.3, purport) Performance of duty is another response to doubt which goes beyond the dialogue of debate. Take to the soothing balm of devotional service and let it work.

Going on pilgrimage to the holy *dhāma*, for intensive hearing and chanting, is a way to combat skeptical doubts. The reality of the spiritual land, the Deities in the temples, and the devotees there will change you.

An important response to doubts is to seek the association of strong devotees. When I first attended the storefront at 26 Second

Avenue, I would have many questions and doubts. Prabhupāda would answer them in his lectures, but then new ones would come to me. But I began to notice that my doubts were answered just by *seeing* Prabhupāda enter the storefront. In the time it took him to walk from the door to his dais, I could feel the doubts being answered. This is the effect of association with a pure devotee.

Preventative Measures

Preventative treatment is better than taking antidotes after you have the disease. Some things to avoid:

1. Indulging in academic studies of Indology or Hinduism. Most of the scholars do not have faith and do not accept that Vedic literature is revealed from a perfect source. Therefore, their skeptical studies can damage a devotional creeper. When I was doing research for *Readings in Vedic Literature*, a *brahmacārī* assisted me by reading extensively in academic Hinduism. As a result, he began to think as they do, that perhaps the Vedic literature is all mythology, and that it was written at a recent time. This caused him a serious relapse. He had to stop the research and recover by chanting and hearing from Prabhupāda's books. It may be necessary to read this literature for specific projects, as some of the ISKCON scholars are doing, but it should be done very carefully. And even if mundane research is required, it should be balanced with equal time for reading in *paramparā*.

2. Skeptical contamination comes not only from direct attacks by Māyāvādīs or atheists. It comes indirectly from secular reading such as *Time* magazine or popular television. Through these sources we begin to breathe the atmosphere of doubt and secularism which is behind them. Although they do not usually "preach,"

their presumption is that we should enjoy sense gratification because we only live once; religion and scriptures are not so important, but rather are old-fashioned things for past ages.

As transcendentalists have always been advised to avoid worldly people and sense enjoyers, so this injunction continues today.

3. A positive approach is to strengthen the mind and spirit by chanting and hearing. Śrīla Prabhupāda writes in the *Bhagavad-gītā*:

> Knowledge in Kṛṣṇa consciousness can be achieved by a faithful person who believes firmly in Kṛṣṇa. One is called a faithful man who thinks that simply by acting in Kṛṣṇa consciousness he can attain the highest perfection. This faith is attained by the discharge of devotional service, and by chanting Hare Kṛṣṇa Hare Kṛṣṇa Kṛṣṇa Kṛṣṇa Hare Hare, Hare Rāma Hare Rāma Rāma Rāma Hare Hare, which cleanses one's heart of all material dirt.
>
> —Bg. 4.39, purport

Once a devotee wrote to Prabhupāda and said that he was having some doubts whether the Vedic literature was universal. Prabhupāda first replied, "May I ask you if you are regularly chanting sixteen rounds of beads? The tricks of the mind or influence of maya will infiltrate if we do not follow the regulative principles and regularly chant the prescribed Names without any offense." (Letter, January 16, 1970)

The Ultimate Solution

Doubts can be countered by bringing them into the open and engaging in dialogue about them. And we should avoid sources of contaminating skepticism. But ultimately the weapons of higher knowledge cannot be useful to us until we gain strength from the Lord Himself. In other words, it is Kṛṣṇa Himself who can vanquish doubts. "Kṛṣṇa or Godhead is light, where there is light, there is not darkness." The Kṛṣṇa sun has to appear in our heart. If we see Kṛṣṇa and know Him, there will be no doubt. "The Supreme Personality of Godhead said: 'Now hear. . . how by practicing *yoga* in full consciousness of Me, with mind attached to Me, you can know Me in full, free from doubt." (Bg. 7.1)

Kṛṣṇa consciousness is not merely an intellectual position, or a political party. It is a state of grace and enlightenment which drives away all ignorance. It is stated in the *Kṛṣṇa* book that the appearance of Kṛṣṇa in the world vanquishes all speculative iconography. People may wonder and doubt about the identity of God, but when He actually appears, then all the doubts go away. Similarly, when Kṛṣṇa appears in your heart and in your life, when you are overflowing with transcendental realization and happiness, then there is no room for doubts. At this stage, you do not have to be a good debater or logician (although such may be used in Kṛṣṇa's service).

Kṛṣṇa appears in the heart by His own grace, but He can be attracted by practices of Kṛṣṇa consciousness and by contact with a pure devotee. The pure devotee defeats doubts not only by his argumentation, but also by the godliness that emanates from his person. Prabhupāda convinced us by arguments, but also by stating, "Kṛṣṇa consciousness is such a nice thing." Coming from him, the words of faith were convincing. As Prabhupāda said of Lord Buddha, "He created faith in the faithless."

Illicit Sex

One time a student of *haṭha-yoga* approached Śrīla Prabhupāda and said, "Although I'm practicing yoga, I have a problem controlling sex desire." Prabhupāda replied, "*You* have a problem? Every living being has that problem." Sex desire in one form or another will continue to appear even within an aspiring devotee until one becomes completely liberated.

Sometimes pious Indian friends find it shocking when devotees mention sex in their lectures, even when it is a *paramparā* discussion. They consider sex to be a forbidden subject, which should not be discussed even for edification. But there is a large amount of information about sex life in Śrīla Prabhupāda's books, and so it should not be avoided. We should not read about sex or discuss it with vicarious enjoyment. But we should hear what the spiritual masters have to say about this powerful force and how to deal with it.

Śrīmad-Bhāgavatam describes why nature created the sex drive and how it should be used.

> The genitals and the pleasure of begetting counteract the distresses of family encumbrances. One would cease to generate altogether if there were not, by the grace of the Lord, a coating, a pleasure-giving substance, on the surface of the generative organs. This substance gives a pleasure so intense that it counteracts fully the distress of family encumbrance. A person is so captivated by this pleasure-giving substance that he is not satisfied by begetting a single child, but increases the number of children, with great risk in regard to maintaining them, simply for this pleasure-giving substance. This pleasure-giving substance is not false, however, because it originates from the transcendental body of the Lord. . . But it has taken on an aspect of pervertedness on account of material contamination.
>
> —*Bhāg*. 2.6.8, purport

The positive use of sex in devotional service is stated concisely by Lord Kṛṣṇa in the *Bhagavad-gītā*, *kāmo 'smi*—"I am sex life which is not contrary to religious principles." (Bg. 7.11) In the purport Prabhupāda writes, "Sex life, according to religious principles *(dharma)*, should be for the propagation of children, not otherwise. The responsibility of parents is then to make their offspring Kṛṣṇa conscious."

Those who do not know the science of transmigration cannot understand the danger of sex attraction. The fact is that it is the greatest binding force for keeping one in the cycle of birth and death.

> Sex is very prominent among animals like monkeys, and such people who are enlivened by sex may be called descendants of

> monkeys. . . They are captivated simply by seeing the faces of one another, which remind them of sense gratification. . . Thus they forget completely that one day their small life span will be finished and they will be degraded in the evolutionary cycle.
>
> —*Bhāg*. 5.14.30–31

Even within marriage, illicit sex drives one to create unwanted pregnancies. This leads to abortion and contraceptives, all of which have karmic reactions.

Śrīla Prabhupāda's standard, the vow of "no illicit sex" which his followers take at initiation, is considered to be extremely strict according to worldly standards. Some even say that he is "denying the basic necessities of life." But the Kṛṣṇa consciousness standard is followed by scriptures and by the founders of bona fide religions all over the world.

> . . . Basically there is no difference between the process of Buddhists, Śaṅkaraites, and Vaiṣṇavaites. For promotion to the highest status of perfection, namely freedom from birth and death, anxiety and fearfulness, not one of these processes allows the follower to break the vow of celibacy.
>
> The householders and persons who have deliberately broken the vow of celibacy cannot enter into the kingdom of deathlessness. The *brahmacārīs*, *vānaprasthas* and *sannyāsīs* do not intend to take rebirth *(apraja)*, nor are they meant for secretly indulging in sex life.
>
> —*Bhāg*. 2.6.20, purport

A typical devotee's experience

We all know the temptation of illicit sex, but devotees also know the strength that comes from Kṛṣṇa consciousness. Every one of us can attest to this to some degree—how we have been relieved of addiction to sex habits.

I can give my own case as an example. When I first met Prabhupāda in 1966, I had typical addictions to sex desire as well as to intoxication. I would try to avoid illicit sex but after some time I would be driven to it. It seemed that unless I enjoyed in that way, my life would be unfulfilled. I was very much influenced by the bombardment of sexuality coming from the entertainment and advertising industries and the strong tide of decadence which was the American norm.

One of the first questions I asked Śrīla Prabhupāda was, "Is there a spiritual advancement you can make from which you don't fall down?" He said "Yes," and by associating with him and chanting with him I began to experience it. Within a few weeks, I was able to give up illicit sex and take the vow. I do not think my case was exceptional. Celibacy is not a pie-in-the-sky. It is not a pathological form of repression. It is the pleasure principle of Kṛṣṇa consciousness that enables us to give up illicit sex.

A devotee in Kṛṣṇa consciousness finds his desire for celibacy enforced by knowledge of the negative results of sex life. Attachment to sex desire makes the soul continue in the cycle of birth and death. I cannot attain pure love for Rādhā and Kṛṣṇa as long as I have material sex desire. In this world, sex is the great "calling card" of *māyā*. It is also described as a shackle which keeps us in material life. These teachings about the negative aspects of illicit sex have a beneficial, sobering effect.

Once we take to Kṛṣṇa consciousness, we see more clearly that sex brings entanglements and sufferings. We do not feel left out for not joining in the tide of addiction to sex. We aspire to remain celibate. But despite all this, sometimes devotees are tempted and sometimes they fall down to illicit sex. It is a formidable obstacle on the path of devotional service.

What Śrīla Prabhupāda Says About Illicit Sex

Śrīla Prabhupāda expected his disciples to be honorable and keep the promises they made at initiation. When devotees wrote to him that they were not following some of the four rules, Prabhupāda never said it was "all right." He said, "You promised at initiation that you would avoid these sinful activities. So you must keep your promise." Śrīla Prabhupāda was convinced that the process of *bhakti-yoga* gave sufficient protection to any of his followers as long as they actually followed.

But Prabhupāda was aware of the weakness of human nature, and he knew that his devotees would sometimes fall down. Lord Kṛṣṇa also acknowledges that devotees make mistakes, especially in the beginning, and He encourages us not to be defeated. Prabhupāda comments:

> . . . An ordinary man with firm faith in the eternal injunctions of the Lord, even though unable to execute such orders, becomes liberated from the law of karma. In the beginning of Kṛṣṇa consciousness, one may not fully discharge the injunctions of the Lord, but because one is not resentful of this principle and works sincerely without consideration of defeat and hopelessness, he will surely be promoted to the stage of pure Kṛṣṇa consciousness.
>
> —Bg. 3.31, purport

The same meaning is found in the well-known verse in the Ninth Chapter, *api cet su-durācāro*, "Even if one commits the most abominable action, if he is engaged in devotional service he is to be considered saintly because he is properly situated in his determination." (Bg. 9.30) Prabhupāda writes, "The material contamination is so strong that even a *yogī* fully engaged in the service of the Lord sometimes becomes ensnared; but Kṛṣṇa consciousness is so strong that such an occasional falldown is at once rectified. . . No one should deride a devotee for some accidental falldown from the ideal path." (Bg. 9.30 purport)

Another example of Prabhupāda's compassion is when he advised persons who had fallen from *sannyāsa* to become respectable *gṛhasthas*. Although, technically speaking, that is not to be recommended, Prabhupāda said the most important thing was to situate yourself in a strong position for fighting *māyā*. Śrīla Prabhupāda was lenient and compassionate, but in none of these statements does he endorse immoral sex. He does not say that we should keep on confessing our wrongs week after week. One who does this is a pseudodevotee.

Prabhupāda usually advised anyone who felt inclinations for sex life to enter the *gṛhastha-āśrama* and act in an honorable way.

> I understand that sometimes you feel sex urges and frustration. In the material world the sex urge is the binding force for material existence. A determined person tolerates such sex urges as one tolerates the itching sensation of eczema. If not one can satisfy the sex urge by legitimate marriage. Immoral sex life and spiritual advancement are incompatible proposition. Your full engagement in K.C. & constant chanting will save you from all inconveniences.
>
> —Letter, January 22, 1968

In this letter Prabhupāda offered me two choices: Either forget sex by engaging twenty-four hours a day in Kṛṣṇa consciousness or enter *gṛhastha* life. But he forbade the third choice, immoral sex.

Prabhupāda wants us to become victorious, and he thinks that it is definitely in our power to do so. He forgives us for occasional mistakes. We should not become guilt-ridden if we have a sex problem that we cannot overcome completely. We should keep trying; we should keep on engaging in devotional service.

But we should not comfort ourselves that everything is all right if we cannot shake sex addiction. It has been clearly stated in the

Śrīmad-Bhāgavatam that one cannot go back to Godhead as long as he has sinful addiction. Neither should we point to the bad examples of those who practice illicit sex and claim, "Everyone is doing it." Kṛṣṇa consciousness is a science, and the material nature also operates under strict laws. We will get the results of our activities.

Avoiding Illicit Sex

How is it possible to avoid all contact with illicit sex since we are living in the "sexual revolution"? It is true that the Vedic teachings were addressed to a more pious audience thousands of years ago. But Śrīla Prabhupāda appeared during the 1970s, and he was well aware of what his students had to contend with. He writes about this in *Śrīmad-Bhāgavatam* while discussing Ajāmila:

> In Kali-yuga, a drunk half-naked woman embracing a drunk man is a very common sight, especially in the Western countries, and restraining oneself after seeing such things is very difficult. Nevertheless, if by the grace of Kṛṣṇa one adheres to the regulative principles and chants the Hare Kṛṣṇa mantra, Kṛṣṇa will certainly protect him. Indeed, Kṛṣṇa says that His devotee is never vanquished (*kaunteya pratijānīhi na me bhaktaḥ praṇaśyati*). Therefore all the disciples practicing Kṛṣṇa consciousness should obediently follow the regulative principles and remain fixed in chanting the holy name of the Lord. Then there need be no fear. Otherwise one's position is very dangerous, especially in this Kali-yuga.
>
> —*Bhāg*. 6.1.60, purport

As a devotee should avoid skeptical and atheistic philosophy in books, he should avoid sex literature, films of illicit sex, and other displays. If you must read a news magazine, why choose one that regularly uses photos of soft pornography? In making deliberate choices like this, one can safeguard the mind. While we cannot walk around with blinders, we can train ourselves in visual discretion and not indulge in second looks at billboards and ads that incite lusty feelings.

There is sometimes only a thin line between observing normal social behavior and protecting yourself from unnecessary exposure to illicit sex. For example, a preacher is expected to be friendly in mixing with women, and women should also greet and speak with male guests on certain occasions. But we also want to observe the injunction that one should not be alone in a secluded place with a woman.

Brahmacārīs and Brahmacāriṇīs

There is also sometimes a thin line between a *brahmacārī's* obligation to protect his celibacy and his obligation to be kind to women devotees. When a *brahmacārī* becomes fanatical in his behavior, he exhibits the "love-hate" syndrome, manifesting attraction to women by displays of hatred for them. A moderate but strict approach is advisable.

When a *brahmacārī* decides to become a *gṛhastha*, is that a falldown? The answer is no. He should be encouraged to take the responsibility for the *āsrama* that is most suitable for him.

However, devotees in the Kṛṣṇa consciousness movement should encourage unmarried men and women to remain celibate if they desire to do so. A *brahmacārī* once wrote to Prabhupāda that the temple president was pressing him to get married. Prabhupāda replied:

> I do not think that Haṁsadūta is pressing you for marriage. Marriage is a concession for a person who cannot control his sex desires. Of course it is a difficult job for the boys in this country because they have free access to intermingling with the girls. Under the circumstances, it is my open order for everyone that everyone can marry without any artificial pose. But if somebody is able to remain a brahmacari, there should not be any causing for his marriage.
>
> . . . Our students, either brahmacari or Householder, are being trained up for constant engagement in Kṛṣṇa consciousness service without any personal interest. This is perfect order of sannyas. So if everyone is trained up in this line of action, all of us are sannyasis in all circumstances.
>
> —Letter, March 7, 1970

Unmarried ladies who aspire for celibacy are encouraged by several verses in the *Śrīmad-Bhāgavatam*, Fifth Canto, spoken by Lakṣmi-devī. She advises all women to accept only Kṛṣṇa as their husband, otherwise one will have to accept a creature made of flesh, blood, mustaches, stool, and urine, a so-called husband who cannot offer his wife any ultimate protection.

Eating and Illicit Sex

There is a connection between one's eating habits and the tendency for sex life. In *Upadeśāmṛta*, the bodily "pushing agents" that should be controlled are the tongue, belly, and genitals. Prabhupāda writes, "One may observe that these three senses are physically situated in a straight line . . . and that the bodily demands begin with the tongue. If one can restrain the demands of the tongue by limiting its activities to eating of *prasāda*, the urges of the belly and the genitals can automatically be controlled." (*Nectar of Instruction*, Text One, purport)

In these same purports Prabhupāda states that even *prasādam*, if overeaten, prepared in too luxurious a manner, or eaten in the mood of sense gratification, can also lead to the uncontrolled tongue—which leads to desire for sex life.

Dreams

There is also a connection between luxurious eating and passing semen in dreams at night. This is not a deliberate act, and so there is no direct action or remedy to prevent it, except for Kṛṣṇa conscious activities. But if one can ascertain a connection between overeating and night pollution, one should take steps to avoid the unconscious sex act.

A *brahmacārī* once wrote to Prabhupāda mentioning unconscious sex agitation and Prabhupāda replied with a down-to-earth suggestion:

> With regard to this problem I recommend that in your diet you take no spices. Furthermore you should see that the bowels are cleared daily.
>
> —Letter, September 22, 1973

If nothing else, sex fantasies while sleeping humble us by revealing that desires for sex indulgence are deeply rooted in the unconscious self. One should not become depressed or guilt-ridden by this (another trick of *māyā*). The best remedy is to fully engage in Kṛṣṇa consciousness with determination to do all that is within one's conscious will to refrain from illicit sex.

The Higher Taste

We have all heard that when we attain the higher taste, sex will seem pale and we will not be interested in it. Śrīla Prabhupāda sometimes gave specific advice for methods which could bring us the higher taste over sex desire. In 1968 a devotee wrote to Prabhupāda saying that he was troubled by "Mr. Lust." Prabhupāda replied:

> Regarding your enemy, Mr. Lust: I have noted the difficulties, but we should always remember that Krishna is stronger than any demon, and Mr. Lust, or his father or his grandfather, nobody can do anything provided we take shelter of Krishna very tightly.

Prabhupāda went on to recommend marriage, although not as a vehicle for exercising lust. Then he recommended Deity worship:

> So to subdue lust is a difficult process. Then you have to take to Deity worship. I am sending herewith one copy of the process of Deity worship. Krishna is Madanamohana. You have already stated in your letter, it is very nice, that you would much prefer to channel all your desire to Krishna, and ask me how is this possible when enveloped in maya, seeing only material forms. You have also written to say that if you can see the Absolute Beauty which is all-attractive, then you could not help but be attracted and would scorn mundane beauty. This is actually the remedy. So you may take immediately to Arcana, the Deity worship. . . . The process is a little difficult in the beginning, but once habituated, it is not at all difficult. So apart from the marriage proposal, you may immediately take to Deity worship. . . And I am sure this process, helped by your regular chanting, will kill Mr. Lust, rest assured. . . . I am at your service always, and give you suggestions and ways and means to make progress in the Deity worship, but you can immediately adopt this principle.
>
> —Letter, October 7, 1968

The Lonely Passion

Masturbation is an illicit form of sex life as described in Prabhupāda's purport in *The Nectar of Instruction:*

> As far as the urges of the genitals are concerned, there are two—proper and improper, or legal and illicit sex. When a man is properly mature, he can marry according to the rules and regulations in the *śāstras* and use his genitals for begetting nice children. That is legal and religious. Otherwise, he may adopt many artificial means to satisfy the demands of the genitals, and he may not use any restraint. When one indulges in illicit sex life, as defined by the *śāstras*, either by thinking, planning, talking about or actually having sexual intercourse, or by satisfying the genitals by artificial means, he is caught in the clutches of *māyā*. These instructions apply not only to householders but also to *tyāgīs*, or those who are in the renounced order of life.
>
> —*Nectar of Instruction*, Text One, purport

There is no reason why this has to be a wide-spread problem among those practicing *bhakti-yoga*. It is not an unconscious act as with dreams, but a deliberate act, and one that does not give real pleasure or any positive result. It is destructive and depressing. Anyone who has this habit should take the responsibility to overcome it and not blame it on anything or anyone else. It is something within your power to stop.

Since masturbation is a deliberate act of the will, it should be stopped as soon as the first stages occur. Acts take place in three stages—thinking, feeling and willing—and so this act, if it is to be stopped at all, has to be stopped in the initial stage.

We should have alert systems within us, similar to military defense systems: As soon as the radar operator sees something dangerous approaching on the radar screen, alarms are set off and the fighters track it down. When I have talked with persons who have this habit, I sometimes ask them where they do it, and what are the circumstances. It often seems to happen when there is particular stress or loneliness or boredom in their life. I suggest that if they find themselves entering the preliminary stages, being in the place where it usually happens, or in the wrong time or state of mind, then they should know right away they are in great danger.

One devotee had this habit from early puberty. He was drawn irresistibly into "adult" book stores. Now he knows that in order to fight his habit, he had to be like the ex-alcoholic who does not even take a drop of liquor. He cannot even allow himself to walk down the same side of the street where there is an adult book store. If one can analyze one's behavior and find the preliminary steps that lead to this unfortunate act, and if one is sincere, he will work hard to stop it. And Kṛṣṇa will help.

I mention the word sincere, but it is a fact that some devotees who *are* sincere still cannot seem to make resolutions strong enough to stop this practice. Therefore it may be necessary for them to adopt a number of changes in their lives. Whatever the changes are, it is worth it.

This particular compulsion is one that can be totally overcome and left behind forever. One of the first steps should be to approach a devotee in whom you trust and confide in him your secret. With his help and with Kṛṣṇa's help, do whatever is necessary to gradually overcome your compulsion. Otherwise, it remains a definite transgression of the principles of illicit sex. Since the devotional life is so pure, a person who masturbates starts to develop great guilt, self-hate, and so on. One does not have to be a professional psychologist in order to see it. Even if we are not able to ascertain the original cause or origin of this habit in a fellow devotee, still we can help each other to overcome it for good. Even in the preliminary stages of devotional service, there is sufficient strength to get rid of the lonely passion.

Homosexuality

We should not think of a person, especially a devotee, as a homosexual. We should not say, "So-and-so dāsa is a homosexual." He is actually a person, a spirit soul. No one is an alcoholic or a psychotic or any other such designation. The conditioned soul may have certain tendencies, including a tendency for homosexuality, but by constitutional nature we are all eternal servants of the Lord, pure and blissful.

When I was a teenager, the first book I ever read about homosexuality described it as a disease. The psychiatrist told how he cured his patients of their homosexual tendency. This view might be considered somewhat old-fashioned, since nowadays people more likely accept the premise that they are homosexually oriented and that such an orientation cannot be changed.

Even if we grant the premise that someone is a homosexual, there is still a course of action if he or she wishes to make advancement in spiritual life. Śrīla Prabhupāda was approached a number of times by devotees who told him of this tendency. His response was that the person should be married. He never endorsed homosexual activity. He used to repeat, with disgust and criticism, a story he had read that a sect in the Christian church gave sanction to homosexual marriage. And he has written in a purport:

> It appears here that the homosexual appetite of males for each other is created in this episode of the creation of the demons by Brahmā. In other words, the homosexual appetite of a man for another man is demoniac and is not for any sane male in the ordinary course of life.
>
> —*Bhāg*. 3.20.26, purport

Śrīla Prabhupāda saw homosexual tendencies as excessive and perverted lust. The legitimate correction for lust is self-control and purification by religious marriage.

If a person of homosexual tendency thinks it is impossible to be married to the opposite sex, then he or she is faced with only one other alternative: celibacy. These are the same two alternatives that Śrīla Prabhupāda wrote to me in a letter when I had mentioned to him of my sex agitation. He said one can either engage oneself fully in Kṛṣṇa consciousness, and thus lose all desire for sex, or become religiously married. But no immoral sex.

A person who has been an active homosexual or feels that he or she is inherently a homosexual should respond to this by accepting a life of full celibacy. The so-called curse can therefore become a blessing.

In order to lead a life of celibacy, such a person may have to make certain adjustments in mixing with persons of the same sex. The same general principle holds: one should not associate intimately with persons with whom one is likely to be sexually attracted. This is true not only of homosexuals but of all celibates. They should avoid genital sex as well as pregenital sexual behavior, and this implies avoiding personal relationships of human affection which are likely to be genitally expressed.

Illicit Sex in Marriage

From time to time we hear rumors of "preaching" in ISKCON that it is not against the rules to enjoy sex intercourse with one's wife even if there is no intention of producing children. To fall a victim to *māyā* is excusable, but it is inexcusable to preach a new "philosophy" that illicit sex in marriage is not a transgression of the initiation vows. Prabhupāda's statements on this are frequent and unequivocal.

As with any sex transgression or any sinful act, occasional slips may be forgiven. But there should be genuine repentance and practical steps taken to overcome it so that it is not repeated. Otherwise the marriage partners will lose respect for each other, and the whole foundation of the Kṛṣṇa conscious marriage can crack to pieces.

Sometimes we hear complaints from a wife or husband that they are being seduced into sex by their spouse. Often it is the women who complain that their husbands force them into illicit sex. They say the husbands demand it in the name of loyalty and submission. But Prabhupāda's instructions about a wife's faithfulness to the husband do not include following a husband who is fallen. If the husband wants to engage in repeated acts of illicit sex, it is not the wife's duty to follow him. Of course the husband's problems also have to be taken into consideration and so compassionate marriage counseling, as well as other attempts to restore a fallen marriage, should be undertaken by the couple.

Here is Prabhupāda's advice to a husband who is about to enter marriage:

> . . . I encourage that all the Brahmacaris may be very responsible and marry one of the girls. Because generally the girls desire good husband and a good home, children, that is their natural propensity, so we want to show some ideal householders also. But the proposal that marriage will solve the question of lust, is not practical. Neither wife should be accepted as a machine for satisfying our lust. The marriage tie should be taken as very sacred. One who marries for subduing lust is mistaken.
>
> —Letter, October 7, 1968

When speaking against these various deviant and illicit sexual acts, devotees should not condemn other persons. Prabhupāda had said we should "hate the sin, not the sinner." The problem should be discussed compassionately, and at the same time the philosophy should not be watered down. In a cool-headed way we should carry out the actual science of Kṛṣṇa consciousness. If you behave rightly you will get the right result; if you behave wrongly you will get another result.

Perhaps some of the remedies I have mentioned are the same things you have heard before. But I hope my discussing it may lead to earnest attempts for reform. We are very fortunate to be able to practice spiritual life, and we should not ruin it by deviant acts.

As we deal with various obstacles on the path of devotional service, we should avoid giving pat philosophical formulas. We should hear out each personal problem and not just mechanically tell people, "Just chant Hare Kṛṣṇa, Prabhu."

One suggestion we repeatedly make is that a devotee ought to confidentially reveal his mind. This may be hard to do with sexual problems, and yet it is also one of the functions of Vaiṣṇava relationships to help each other in this way. One of the conditions of such exchanges is that they should be confidential. We should find a person whom we can talk with openly and admit falldowns or addictions. That person should be trustworthy, and there should not be intimidation or wrong motivation in the relationship. When the conditions are right, then just by admitting our weakness we will make progress.

Obstacles in Chanting and Reading

According to *Śrīmad-Bhāgavatam*, *all* obstacles can be overcome by one who regularly chants and hears the message of the Supreme Personality of Godhead:

> Living beings who are entangled in the complicated meshes of birth and death can be freed immediately by even unconsciously chanting the holy name of Kṛṣṇa. . . . Who is there, desiring deliverance from the vices of the age of quarrel, who is not willing to hear the virtuous glories of the Lord?
>
> —*Bhāg*. 1.1.14; 16

The *Bhāgavatam* also speaks of cutting the knot in the heart. This knot, *hṛdaya-granthi*, is the total of all our false attachments to the self and the world. If that knot (false ego) is untied by the Supreme Lord, then one realizes the happiness of the self.

Śrīla Prabhupāda also used the metaphor of hurdles which appear on the path. He writes, "The transcendental name of Kṛṣṇa, even though uttered unconsciously or by force of circumstances, can help one obtain freedom from the hurdles of birth and death." (*Bhāg.* 1.1.14, purport)

Chanting and hearing about Kṛṣṇa is also compared to "switching on the light of pure knowledge within the heart of the devotees." When the Supreme Himself takes charge of illuminating the heart of the devotee, then one cannot remain in darkness.

The *śāstras* also compare the removal of material obstacles to cleaning away dirt. This is done primarily by the process of *śravaṇam* and *kīrtanam*.

> Śrī Kṛṣṇa, the Personality of Godhead, who is the Paramātmā (Supersoul) in everyone's heart and the benefactor of the truthful devotee, cleanses desire for material enjoyment from the heart of the devotee who has developed the urge to hear His messages, which are in themselves virtuous when properly heard and chanted.
>
> —*Bhāg.* 1.2.17

Who can fail to be moved by these statements? He must be stone-hearted. Who will not chant and hear the glories of the Lord, after hearing the praises of *śravaṇam kīrtanam* as given in *Śrīmad-Bhāgavatam*? His ears are no better than the holes snakes crawl into. His voice is no better than the croaking of the frog, who calls to attract death.

Despite the Vedic promises that Kṛṣṇa removes all problems when we chant and hear, it is not uncommon for initiated devotees to become slack in these primary practices. Does this mean that the descriptions of the glories of *śravaṇam kīrtanam* are false advertisements? A sincere devotee will never accept such a blasphemous statement. And yet on a personal basis, devotees sometimes have doubts whether *śravaṇam kīrtanam* will actually work *for them*. Despite vows to chant at least sixteen rounds a day, many give it up, or reduce the required quota. The reading of Prabhupāda's books is also sometimes given up, or reduced to an occasional glance. In cases like these, it is not hard to understand that the obstacles in the path of devotional service are primarily caused by the lack of chanting and hearing. Therefore, the most dangerous obstacle of all is when we neglect the very things that brings us release from the knots in the heart.

What's Wrong?

Why do we fail to find taste, why do we lose the discipline to perform chanting and hearing as a daily duty of life? In the *Hari-nāma Cintāmaṇi*, Bhaktivinoda Ṭhākura analyzes this difficulty in regard to inattentive chanting of the holy names. He states that if a neophyte devotee is not very scrupulous in taking up the practices of chanting and hearing, he will quickly grow distracted, and this will produce "a type of illusion, causing serious offenses against the holy name that are very difficult to overcome." What happens is that one simply gives up interest in the pursuit of spiritual life and turns his attention to cravings for wealth, sex and fame. "When these attractions cover the heart, the neophyte gradually loses interest in chanting of the holy name." Realized in this way, the failure to pursue the two main practices of *bhakti* (*śravaṇam kīrtanam*) is not due to the omission of a particular detail, and it is certainly not the fault of the process of *bhakti* itself. The fault is in ourselves. We have become weak-hearted, and so *māyā* has entered once again and turned our heads. We do not want to chant and hear about the Lord because we are absorbed in sense gratification.

A good beginning for *japa* and reading reform is to accept this blunt analysis of why we are not interested in *śravaṇaṁ kīrtanam.* Let me admit, "I'm not interested in chanting because I have too many material desires." This is humbling, and it is the truth. I could offer more intricate and psychological reasons, and even circumstantial explanations, excuses and rationalizations, but it is better to reach the bedrock: acceptance of our causeless unwillingness to serve the Supreme Lord. Now we will be in a better position to consider the grave dangers of material life and to recall why we were attracted to Kṛṣṇa consciousness in the first place.

There will never be a clearer analysis of why we cannot chant nicely than the explanation and remedy given by Rūpa Gosvāmī in the *Upadeśāmṛta:*

> The holy name, character, pastimes and activities of Kṛṣṇa are all transcendentally sweet like sugar candy. Although the tongue of one afflicted by the jaundice of avidyā (ignorance) cannot taste anything sweet, it is wonderful that simply by carefully chanting these sweet names every day, a natural relish awakens within his tongue, and his disease is gradually destroyed at the root.
>
> —*Nectar of Instruction*, Text 7

Rūpa Gosvāmī's verse is worth putting on a 3" x 5" card in a place where we can see it every day—and not just see it, but feel it.

Where's the Nectar?

A disappointed practitioner might complain, "Your explanation is philosophically correct, but you haven't dealt with the nitty-gritty problem. How can we chant if we don't have a taste?" Many of us have heard pat philosophical explanations as to what is wrong with our chanting, but it does not change our hearts or move us into reform. We admit to our fallen state. It does not make us happy to put aside our chanting beads, to read *Time* rather than *Śrīmad-Bhāgavatam*. We wish that we could chant better, and we know that it is a main obstacle in our life. But we do not know how to overcome it.

If we have lost a taste for chanting and hearing, it is unreasonable that we demand an immediate return of the taste *before* we try to improve ourselves. We have to go through a process in order to regain health. We cannot expect the ripened fruit of blissful chanting to suddenly drop from the sky, and we should not wait until material life gets so bad that we turn in hopeful desperation to the shelter of chanting and hearing. With whatever little abilities we have now, let us revive determination to follow the vows for chanting and hearing.

I am speaking of the old virtues, faith and determination. Perhaps these virtues have worn thin for you because someone misled you in the name of faith and determination. Or maybe you are tired of trying without attaining a higher taste. If we chant and hear only because of duty, it will become routine and mechanical. And so we demand, "Where is the nectar?" But for one who has not yet qualified for tasting *bhakti-rasa*, the duty of *sādhana-bhakti* should never be derided. Yes, in Goloka Vṛndāvana, there is no longer any duty. *There* everything is spontaneous; walking is dancing, speech is song, and the *surabhī* cows give endless milk. By contrast, the austerities of the *sādhaka* (the practitioner of devotional service) may strike us as demeaning. But experts in devotional service, such as Rūpa Gosvāmī and Śrīla Prabhupāda, encourage us, saying that the path to *bhakti-rasa* goes through the progressive stages of *sādhana-bhakti*.

A sincere *sādhana-bhakta* will learn to worship the duties given to him by the spiritual master, and he will find nectar in carrying out the instructions for chanting and hearing. "I know I am doing the best thing for my spiritual progress and happiness. Let me be patient." Although we may not experience the eight kinds of transcendental ecstasies, if we think about it, we will admit that we *have* experienced deep and abiding pleasures in chanting and hearing. These pleasures and this auspiciousness are as close to us as the touch of our *japa* beads, and the reading of the book on the shelf.

Be Willing to Change

One suggestion of an overall nature is that one should *be willing to make changes in one's life in order to give* sādhana *a chance to survive*. For example, if a business firm discovers that it is in financial difficulty, then the members sit down and decide on appropriate action. This may require sacrifices and changes. Everything cannot stay the way it is. The willingness to sit down, discuss, and bring about changes is a prerequisite. Otherwise, friends may offer you many suggestions for improving your chanting and hearing, but you will not budge an inch. As Śrīla Prabhupāda has said, if one wants to keep everything the way it is, then he cannot help himself in devotional service.

What are some of the changes that may be required? Perhaps we are living with people who make it impossible to pursue devotional service. Maybe our means of making money is too hellish, sapping our vital energy so that we have no inclination left for spiritual practices. Or there may be unresolved grudges in our life. As Jesus Christ says, "If you are going to make an offering on the altar, but you remember that you have cheated someone, first go and make peace with that person, then come back and make your offering."

Maybe we have to move into a temple community in order to chant. Or maybe we have to move out of the temple. What has to be done will vary with each person. But *some* adjustment in favor of *sādhana* has to be considered and actually carried out. Maybe it means we have to make less money. Maybe we have to move our place of residence. Or after considering, we may think that there is really no external change that is necessary: "It's just a matter of my own will power." But that in itself is a major change or adjustment. We have to agree, "All right, I'm going to do the needful."

We may conclude that we will be able to give 2 1/2 hours a day to *japa*, and 1/2 hour a day for reading Prabhupāda's books. If that is our decision, then the next step is to ensure that even this small amount of time for *bhajana* is kept sacred. We have to be in a decent state of mind to actually chant and hear. *Śravaṇaṁ kīrtanam* requires mental peace and alertness. If the hours which we spend away from *sādhana* are too passionate or demanding, they will leave us burned out. We will be too exhausted or contaminated to utilize the little time left for chanting and hearing. We cannot run at a greyhound's pace twenty-two hours a day and then suddenly screech to a stop and switch into the mode of *sattva-guṇa*. If we have allowed ourselves to become like dogs working at *ugrākarma;* if we have allowed ourselves to become trapped in a life with high stress in order to maintain a standard of living; if we are always fighting with our wife or husband; if we are engaged in an extramarital sexual affair; if we are plotting and scheming to get ahead or cheat someone—this will ruin whatever little time we have scheduled for *sādhana*.

So the plans for change may have to go deep. And if we are part of a family, it will have to be done in cooperation with others, so that everyone's material and spiritual needs are satisfied.

What's the Best Way to Read?

Even if our lives are relatively peaceful, we have to give ourselves a little preparation before practicing *japa* or reading. It may take only a moment to remind ourselves, "Now I'm going to chant the Lord's holy names," or, "Now I'm going to read a very special book, *Śrīmad-Bhāgavatam*. Let me do it with reverence and submission. This is not ordinary reading."

We should be aware that there *is* a transition from ordinary consciousness to speaking and hearing transcendental sound vibration. You cannot open the *Bhagavad-gītā* as you would a newspaper and start scanning it or cramming. It will not work. First, you have to calm yourself and enter a state of worship. Only then can you actually read or chant. "Before reciting this *Śrīmad-Bhāgavatam*, which is the very means of conquest, one should offer respectful obeisances unto the Personality of Godhead, Nārāyaṇa, unto Nara-nārāyaṇa Ṛṣi, the supermost human being, unto mother Sarasvatī, the goddess of learning, and unto Śrīla Vyāsadeva, the author." (*Bhāg.*1.2.4)

Devotees have to develop their own methods of preparing their consciousness for *sādhana*. The best method is in Kṛṣṇa's advice, "Just fix your mind upon Me, the Supreme Personality of Godhead, and engage all your intelligence in Me. Thus you will live in Me always, without a doubt." (Bg. 12.8) But Lord Kṛṣṇa is aware that many persons are "too busy" or harassed to stay in a continuous flow of devotional meditation. So Kṛṣṇa recommends, "If you cannot fix your mind upon Me without deviation, then follow the regulative principles of *bhakti-yoga*. In this way develop a desire to attain Me." (Bg. 12.9) This implies a deliberate turning away from other thoughts to the practice of Kṛṣṇa consciousness, which we do when we take up chanting and hearing.

One devotee makes this transition by first reading a few of his favorite *ślokas* while accompanying himself on the *tamboura*.

Someone else first places the book on his head in reverence, and another offers flowers to the book. For *japa*, some devotees bow down to the ground and recite the Pañca-tattva mantra before beginning to chant Hare Kṛṣṇa.

It will be easier to make this transition if we perform our *sādhana* regularly. If I chant at the same time every day and in the same place, it will be easier to discipline the mind. And because I have arranged a time when I am not likely to be disturbed, I will be able to carry out my plans.

There is a special advantage in the early hours of the day, *brahmā-muhūrta*. We do not have to stop in the middle of passionate activities as we would in midday. Business activities have not started. It is a new day.

Aside from arranging a daily schedule that is favorable to *sādhana*, we might also consider special times during the year which we can devote to chanting and hearing. Usually we go on pilgrimage to India for this purpose. But when we finally do get to India, we often find ourselves involved mostly in shopping, or getting sick, or meeting devotees from all over the world. It might be best to schedule a visit to India during an off-season, or even schedule a visit to some other place in the world, where we can be peaceful and devote ourselves to chanting and hearing. This kind of intensive work over a period of days or weeks can do a lot to help us overcome the obstacle of mechanical chanting and reading.

There are also methods of reading that make it more favorable for entering the devotional state. One favorable method is to read more slowly and prayerfully. It is not important to finish whole chapters or whole books. (This is especially true for those who have read all of Prabhupāda's books several times.) The important thing is to enter the spirit of even a single verse. Prabhupāda has said that if we could understand one verse of *Śrīmad-Bhāgavatam*, or one word in a verse, our lives would become perfect. Prayerful reading brings one into a personal relationship with the speaker of the verses, Lord Kṛṣṇa and His pure devotees. We speak to Kṛṣṇa with our prayers of intention, and then we listen to Him as He speaks in the *śāstra*.

Slow meditative reading is not the only way to read. Sometimes we will want to *study*, taking notes. Sometimes we want to relax as we read. There are no hard and fast rules in chanting or reading, so we should do whatever works for us. Two or more friends can come together to read *Śrīmad-Bhāgavatam* and base their conversation on the contents of the verses and purports. Or we might want to sit with a friend or family member while each of us reads silently. If we start to practice we will find methods of our own inclination, and our interest will grow stronger.

Confessions of a Poor Japa Chanter

One who attempts to write a book called "Obstacles on the Path of Devotional Service" runs the risk of sounding like an all-knowing teacher. This is not the case with me, and so I would like to admit to my own struggles in chanting *japa*. I have not neglected the vow to chant sixteen rounds a day. But I confess that I am unable to appreciate the holy names. When I say this, some of my friends think that I am being humble and that actually I am tasting the holy name very blissfully. One friend took me more seriously yet said that perhaps Kṛṣṇa is withholding the nectar of the holy name from me so that I can sympathize with the struggles of others! Some who have heard my confession conclude that I must be what I say I am, backward. But they do not like to hear my admissions. "What's his problem? Why can't he just chant like everybody else?" Other friends have pointed out to me that according to *śāstra*, I am committing *nāma-aparādhas*, and that is why I do not have a taste for the holy names.

While accepting this failure, I also wish to share a conviction I have of the importance of performing duty, despite the failure. To me, the bottom line is duty. My spiritual master told me to chant Hare Kṛṣṇa, and so I will never give it up. I do not regard this duty as a nonsense thing. It is all I have, and so it's very dear to me. I also have become aware that it may take a long time for me to "master" the art of chanting Hare Kṛṣṇa. It is not something easily attained. This thought helps me to become more patient. So what if I have been chanting for twenty-five years? Maybe in five years from now it will become more clear to me. It is up to Kṛṣṇa. And it also depends on my desire.

I take solace in the statements by Prabhupāda that devotional service is a slow process. Like everyone else, sometimes I feel better about chanting than at other times. Sometimes I'm very worried that I should do better, and sometimes I'm patient and easy on myself. Sometimes I thank Kṛṣṇa for the wonderful gift of the holy name, and sometimes I beg for His mercy so that I may chant in earnest. (Sometimes I alternate this thanking and begging within the space of a single mantra: "Thank You!—please have mercy!")

Devotees report that when they do feel they are improving in their chanting, this often results in pride that everything is going well. Then they fall again into a valley of inattentive chanting. Maybe we should *always* feel very fallen and humble. When we feel very fallen, we are actually chanting in a way that is pleasing to Kṛṣṇa. It may not even be advisable to try to figure out where I am on the devotional chart of progress. The all-important thing is to keep trying with determination and faith. We are as close to Kṛṣṇa as possible when we chant the holy name. Although we cannot imitate Lord Caitanya, we can follow His mood: "When will the day come when by chanting, tears will flow from My eyes, and My voice will choke up at the utterance of the holy name?"

And so we return to the same conclusion, that all obstacles on the path can be removed by chanting and hearing. Even if we cannot solve other problems, we must tackle the obstacle of neglecting the basic *sādhana*, *śravaṇaṁ kīrtanam*. And as soon we begin, we will be encouraged in the efficacy of these practices:

> Śri Kṛṣṇa, the Personality of Godhead, who is the Paramātmā (Supersoul) in everyone's heart and the benefactor of the truthful devotee, cleanses desire for material enjoyment from the heart of the devotee who has developed the urge to hear His messages, which are in themselves virtuous when properly heard and chanted.
>
> —*Bhāg*. 1.2.17

Physical Illness

Some devotees, especially those who are young, may consider physical illness to be a specialized topic, of interest only to a few. Not so many devotees may have had prolonged illness. But in fact, illness is one of the main problems of material life, along with birth, death, and old age. Sooner or later these four miseries come to everyone.

During the last days of his illness in 1977, Śrīla Prabhupāda said to a *sannyāsī* at his beside, "Don't think this won't happen to you." If at present we are healthy, there will come a time when we will be ill. We are sometimes rich, sometimes poor; sometimes happy, sometimes sad; sometimes a human being, and sometimes in the species of birds or beasts. And so we will have our turn to become ill. One who laughs at the physically ill may be reminded of the parable of the wet and dry pieces of dung. A piece of wet stool laughed to see a piece of dry dung hurled into the fire. (In India, when cow dung dries it is used in fire as fuel). The wet stool could not comprehend that as soon as he dried off, he also would be thrown into the fire.

A temporary illness may be merely bothersome, or it can turn into a crisis in spiritual life whereby one loses his desire to perform devotional service. But even the most severe physical disease, when accepted in a Kṛṣṇa conscious way, can bring many benefits.

Prabhupāda on Illness

What did Śrīla Prabhupāda say about devotees' illness? He was concerned and compassionate; he used to sign all his letters, "Hope this meets you in good health." In Śrīla Prabhupāda's early letters, he often recommended home remedies for illness, and he suggested that devotees take good care of their bodies as instruments in Kṛṣṇa's service.

"As you are sick with the flu now," he wrote to a disciple in 1969, "I think it is best that you do not exert yourself by working too much strenuously but rather you rest as much as possible until you are feeling better." (Letter, January 16, 1969)

Śrīla Prabhupāda taught that Kṛṣṇa conscious life provided its own system of hygiene, including a balanced diet, exercise, rest, and optimistic mentality.

Ever since Śrīla Prabhupāda first came to America in 1965, he contended with his own illness associated with old age. From his own experience, he directed his disciples.

> Physically and mentally we may be disturbed sometimes, but we have to stand erect on the spiritual platform. I may inform

> you in this connection that I am at the moment physically unfit; I am having always a buzzing sound in my brain. I cannot sleep soundly at night, but still I am working because I try to be in position of spiritual platform. I hope you shall try to understand me right and do the needful.
>
> —Letter, January 15, 1968

Prabhupāda did not endorse a particular school of medicine or put full faith in medical panaceas. Neither did he say that doctors should be avoided. He advised that devotees take normal measures for recovery but mainly depend on Kṛṣṇa by chanting Hare Kṛṣṇa.

One time when Śrīla Prabhupāda was lecturing on the twenty-six qualities of a devotee, he commented that "a devotee is friendly." He said that when fellow devotees become sick, we should be very sympathetic to them and take care of them. The devotees are somewhat like soldiers in battle. When one of them gets sidelined, he or she sometimes has the unfortunate experience of being neglected. As ISKCON matures, it will give more emphasis to the care of the ill and aged workers of the movement.

My Story

I would like to share some of my experiences of a prolonged illness. It came as a shock to me when suddenly I could not do my normal duties. At first you do not want to accept it. You keep trying to act normally, but the material nature forces you to the floor and you have to submit.

As you lie in your sickbed, you worry that perhaps you are not actually sick. Maybe you are a malingerer. You have heard that most diseases are psychosomatic, and you wonder exactly what that means. Maybe you are not being sincere enough. You try again to get up and disregard your illness, but you are rudely thrown down. After going through this struggle for a while, you accept the fact that you are sincere about wanting to be well. You wish to serve your spiritual master's mission, but the fact is, you cannot do it now. You have to deal with your physical illness and not feel guilty about it. This is a mental problem that comes along with physical disease.

The fear of being seen as a malingerer is related to a social image. You make heroic efforts to act as if you are not ill because you're afraid of what others will think or say about you. Śrīla Prabhupāda said that devotees should be sympathetic, but we cannot expect everyone to be preoccupied with our disease. We have to take care of ourselves.

With the aid of close friends, we take to medical treatment and a health regimen. But while we rest in bed, we worry that some devotees are expecting us to be active and they are disappointed in us. Someone may even think that we are "in *māyā*." If anyone inquires from us with an unsympathetic attitude, we have to tolerate this and inform them politely that we are not in *māyā;* we are simply taking care of our illness. This is an extra burden for the ill: to live in a society of people who are active and who cannot always understand and sympathize.

The ill person has to accept the fact that he may be losing his popularity. The book distributor who becomes ill is no longer praised daily for his record-breaking feats. People begin to forget about you. You no longer feel the satisfaction that you are doing something worthwhile in Lord Caitanya's mission. Of course, the truth goes deeper than this, and yet a diseased person sometimes suffers disappointments because of these changes in his life.

Next comes the humbling realization that you are not that much needed. You may have been a leading preacher, but Kṛṣṇa will send someone else to do your work. Everything does not collapse just because you are not on the scene. On the one hand it is a solace to learn that your work is being covered by others. But it is also humiliating. You had thought that many people were depending on you, but new people are coming forward and taking your place. Although a few visitors give you flowers, you are not terribly missed. But to dwell on these things is a needless worry that does not help your physical illness.

"I Cannot Chant My Rounds"

So you cannot do the big work that you used to do when you were healthy. Face it. But what if your illness is one that prevents you from the simplest and most basic service, chanting your sixteen rounds? It often happens that a physically sick person cannot chant due to nausea or pain, or the doctor's drugs. When the days and weeks drag on like that, devotees get worried. They fall behind in their vow to chant sixteen rounds daily. How will they ever make it up? But there is no benefit in adding anxiety to the illness we already have. We should not think that Kṛṣṇa is holding it against us if we cannot chant so well when we're ill. He will understand and forgive us.

If we cannot chant sixteen healthy rounds, that does not mean that we should give up all effort. Instead of rising early and vigorously chanting sixteen rounds before *maṅgala-ārati*, we may have to find a new way to do it. Maybe we can only chant very softly, or we may have to chant in the mind. Chanting is our most important service of the day, and so we should continue to try. If we are not experiencing intense pain, we can chant at least a few rounds, even if that constitutes our entire day's *sādhana*. And if we cannot attend the morning program in the temple, then we can have our own program in bed, with a minimum of chanting and hearing, according to our capacity.

In conditions where we cannot even chant properly, then our duty is to remain in good consciousness, as far as possible. Be peaceful, chant as much as you can, and hear about Kṛṣṇa. When I was ill, some of my friends made recordings of themselves reading from Prabhupāda's books. I used to hear those tapes for many hours a day. It became an important service for me to stay awake and hear the readings. You learn to accept whatever little service you can do, and you treasure it.

You are out of the mainstream of the *saṅkīrtana* movement. Everything continues;. The marathon continues, the festivals continue, the fight between the demons and the devotees continues—but you are sidelined. You may hear about what's happening, and some things you do not even hear about. You live in a small world where you chant a few rounds, read a little, sleep, and try to get better. But *that* is your holy service, and so you accept it in a humble way. Eventually you begin to feel something nice and sweet. There is an advantage you can feel in your reduced state. You are being humbled.

While I was ill, I wrote this little poem:

My list of things to do
falls to the side.
All I do is rest.
But one cry to Kṛṣṇa
is worth a hundred steps
of marching in pride.

Pray for Health?

Another consideration is whether you should pray to Lord Kṛṣṇa for health. The desire to pray for Prabhupāda's health was shared by all devotees during his last year. We all wanted him to become well. He was not traveling, and he could not work full-time on his books. We heard that maybe he would leave this world, and so we wanted to pray to Kṛṣṇa and make Prabhupāda better. Prabhupāda's secretary remarked to Prabhupāda, "Lord Balarāma is so powerful, it wouldn't be a difficult thing for him to make you well." Prabhupāda agreed that if Kṛṣṇa desired he could get better. Devotees wrote to Prabhupāda asking if they could exchange their youth and health for Prabhupāda's old age. Hearing their strong sentiments, Prabhupāda permitted the devotees to pray to Kṛṣṇa for his health. The prayer he gave us was, "My dear Lord Kṛṣṇa, if You desire, please cure Śrīla Prabhupāda." (We may note the phrase, "If You desire".)

Should we use the full force of our faith to ask for physical health? Some religionists take it as a sign of their potency or faith in God that when they pray to Him in illness, He cures their physical disease. But Kṛṣṇa conscious devotees are not faith healers.

A devotee knows that he has become ill due to *karma*, or at least he is getting token reaction of *karma*. He wants to accept gladly whatever Kṛṣṇa sends, and he tries to understand everything as Kṛṣṇa's plan. This is expressed in the *Bhāgavatam* verse, *tat te 'nukampāṁ su samīkṣa-māṇo* . . .

> My dear Lord, one who earnestly waits for You to bestow Your causeless mercy upon him, all the while patiently suffering the reactions of his past misdeeds and offering You respectful obeisances with his heart, words and body, is surely eligible for liberation, for it has become his rightful claim.
>
> —*Bhāg*. 10.14.8

One of Prabhupāda's senior disciples, Gobhatta dāsa of Santo Domingo, told me the realization he gained about *karma* after a car accident left him crippled for life. After the accident, Gobhatta entered a hospital ward which he shared with other patients who also had life-crippling injuries. Gobhatta was told by the psychologist there that the main problem for patients like him was to face the agonizing question, "*Why did this happen to me?*" But Gobhatta Prabhu said, "That thought never passed my mind, not even for a moment." He realized that his suffering must have been due to some reaction of past activities, and so he did not need to figure out a "why." Although he experienced the same physical difficulties as the other patients, he did so in the spirit of *tat te 'nukampāṁ* and was able to avoid extreme depression.

Silver Linings

I found some "silver linings" in the clouds of my illness. Although I had become a semi-invalid with chronic headaches, I was fortunate to be able to stay in a cabin in the woods at Gītā-nāgarī. My main "activity" day and night was to lie in bed. But I was able to go out at least briefly each day to take a walk on a forest path. Through the spring and summer I gradually allowed myself to become attracted to nature. I noticed wild flowers and wild plants, the trees and the birds. At first I was hesitant to fall in love with nature, thinking it might be *māyā*. Can a devotee be a nature-lover? But I began to hear Prabhupāda speaking of nature on tapes. He assured me that a devotee sees Kṛṣṇa in nature. I remained hesitant and wrote about it in my diary:

> Early this morning from within my room I heard the songs of several different birds. One I knew was a robin. Baladeva said that there was also a nuthatch. Their songs lifted my spirits, and when I opened the curtains, I saw a pair of ducks sailing swiftly downstream in the rain-filled creek.
>
> I should be careful that I do not become a worshiper of the Universal Form (seeing flowers as Kṛṣṇa's smile, birds as His

> song etc.). Beyond the Viśvarūpa conception is the topmost spiritual engagement of chanting the holy name, as given by Lord Caitanya. So in an ultimate sense, endeavoring to see God in Nature is supplementary to these other spiritual activities. Yet, even now, in this very body, at my very door, I am seeing little bits of Kṛṣṇa, and that should not be discounted.

I felt fortunate to be able to write about nature and share it with the devotees. I knew they could not make nature appreciation their full-time engagement, but if I could share what had inspired me, it could be a way to serve the devotees.

As weeks and months went by, I became more attuned to nature and more confident. It was one of the few areas of expression that Kṛṣṇa allowed me in my physical illness.

> Today the wind blows strongly, and a large flotilla of mustard garlic leaves, yellowed and dead, moves downstream. I watched a delicate rabbit devour the leaves of a wild cabbage. The morning sky was overcast, but now the sun breaks through the clouds, creating dramatic lighting—bright sparkles on the rapids, shadows from the trees. Boughs are swaying, leaves dancing, and a ruffling fills the air.
>
> In the cabin, about a dozen vases, each with a single rose flower, are sitting in a row before Jagannātha, Subhadrā, and Baladeva, for Their pleasure. Going out for five minutes to pick flowers is one of the few things the doctor has allowed me to do this week.

Another silver lining that came to me while I was ill was that I was forced to spend more time alone. Before my breakdown, I was very active in meeting people all day long and traveling all over the world. My attention was filled up with the challenges of life in ISKCON. If I thought of solitude at all, I regarded it as a kind of sense gratification. There was so much to be done to help other people by spreading Kṛṣṇa consciousness, so there was no reason to be alone. But when I *had to* be alone because of illness, I gradually began to appreciate it. There is, of course, a danger in that you may indulge in solitude and withdraw from the world. I do not say that I escaped completely from that indulgence. And yet I considered it a great benefit to learn more of the introspective and thoughtful aspects of a human life.

There is more to spiritual life than meeting people and giving people books. There is also a time for thinking about Kṛṣṇa. Kṛṣṇa says that the best of all *yogis* is one who is "always absorbed in Me and thinks of Me within himself." Kṛṣṇa also says that we should experience life within; do not think that happiness comes only by contact of the senses with the world. When you are an invalid, you learn to face yourself.

I took up diary writing at this time, and it became a form of preaching or *kirtana* for me. Even if one is not inclined to write, he will naturally start to think more when he lives alone. You review your whole life, consider how you have been superficial and how you have hurt people. You think of your mistakes, and you try to turn more to Kṛṣṇa. You do this because there is nothing else you can do. If this happens during your confined state, then you have found a valuable silver lining to your illness.

A healthy person does not want to remain sick and inactive. We have important work to do. The Kṛṣṇa consciousness movement could not continue if everyone was in a sickbed. And yet one at a time, each of us becomes sick. So instead of being completely miserable and distressed in mind, or "spacing out"—instead of thinking of yourself as a lump of mucus, or a big ball of pain, you have to find yourself within that situation, and find the silver lining.

Keeping a Balance

There is a balance that has to be kept in illness. We should be sincere, not pretending just to get some attention. But there *is* such a thing as hypochondria, and so we may ask ourselves, "How do I know that I am not babying myself?" One answer to this is to follow a health regimen to the best of your ability. In most cases, allopathic treatment with its reliance on drugs is not very good for a devotee. But we should follow some regimen and try to put our faith in it. It is a way of showing Kṛṣṇa that we are really trying to get better. We are not babying ourselves, but we are following a strict diet and being a good patient. Our regimen may include physical therapy and patience, and so we take it on as our service. By obedience to a regimen, we avoid falling into a pit of helpless illness. We do what we can in a cheerful mood and wait to see what Kṛṣṇa desires. If our doctors and advisers suggest that we try to be more active, we should not prefer to remain in bed. By making little attempts to recover whenever possible, we will prove that we are not hypochondriacs. If we try to act as if we were well but find that we are still ill, then we should also accept that as Kṛṣṇa's mercy.

Depression

When illness is prolonged or painful, we have to restrict ourselves from becoming depressed. Depression is another of *māyā's* tricks. Śrīla Prabhupāda has described how a devotee should not indulge in depression.

> Instead of employing enthusiasm for attaining material goals, one should be enthusiastic about achieving the perfectional

> stage of devotional service. Indeed, enthusing His devotees in devotional service is the purpose for which Kṛṣṇa descends to this material world.
>
> If one, however, becomes disappointed in his enthusiasm for serving the Supreme Lord, that disappointment must also be restricted.
>
> The devotee should patiently follow the rules and regulations of devotional service so that the day will come when he will achieve, all of a sudden, all the perfection of devotional service.
>
> —*Nārada-bhakti Sūtra*, Code 5, purport

When we are young and enjoying with our senses, eating and tasting and running about, we are actually more in illusion than we are when we are sick in bed. When we are faced with the painful situation of the body—"this material body is a lump of ignorance"—we do not like it, and we want to get well as soon as possible. Yet illness does teach us that the material body is inherently "a network of paths unto death." So illness can teach us dependence on Kṛṣṇa.

All things considered, illness is misery. Lord Kṛṣṇa says that we should tolerate bodily miseries which come and go like summer and winter seasons. We should maintain stability and go on with our duty to become Kṛṣṇa conscious. We should not become critical of those who find fault with us, and neither should we fall in lethargy. Even if our duties are simply those of the sickbed, we can keep the bed clean, and go through the routine activities of illness in a way that is conducive to the modes of goodness. Although we cannot cure our physical illness, we can remain cheerful as we follow our very limited program. If our duty is to tolerate miseries and to chant a little bit each day—and to accept the fact that we are each a tiny devotee—then this is the challenge we have to meet. This is how we can cope with the misery of physical disease.

Obstacles Presented by the Nondevotee World

According to the Vedic scriptures, three-fourths of all spirit souls are liberated and living in the eternal spiritual world. But on the earth planet, it is very rare to find a spirit soul who is aspiring for pure devotional service. Lord Kṛṣṇa gives the statistics: "Out of many thousands among men, one may endeavor for perfection, and of those who have achieved perfection, hardly one knows Me in truth." (Bg. 7.3) Devotees should not feel sorry that they are such a small minority. Śrīla Prabhupāda has encouraged us not to seek the endorsement of the *vox populi*, and he also said that we should be callous toward the scorn of the nondevotees. But it is natural that a practicing devotee sometimes feels sensitive if he or she is laughed at for wearing Vaiṣṇava dress, or if one is seen as a weird cult member. These inimical attitudes create an obstacle on the path of devotional service.

Worldly pressures may be especially difficult in the beginning, when one is trying to decide if he or she wants to join the Kṛṣṇa consciousness movement. One has to break away from friends and sometimes even family members. When George Harrison was very interested in practicing Kṛṣṇa consciousness, he admitted to Śrīla Prabhupāda that his interest in Kṛṣṇa was causing him to lose friends. Prabhupāda encouraged him to continue in Kṛṣṇa consciousness, but social pressure was at least part of the reason why George found it impossible to commit himself to Kṛṣṇa consciousness.

Even those who become initiated continue to see worldly opposition as an obstacle to their devotional service. There are so many prejudices against devotees, especially in Western countries. You may not be able to buy a house if the owners know that you are a practicing Vaiṣṇava, and you may not be able to get a job unless you conceal your religion. A predisposed enmity against "Hare Kṛṣṇas" has been discovered by courts of justice when they attempt to select a jury in cases involving members of the Kṛṣṇa consciousness movement. The anti-cult movement continues its war of propaganda, in which devotees of Kṛṣṇa are characterized as pathological, anti-social and dangerous. Devotees may do their best to offset these images, but who can say that he is completely undisturbed in the face of opposition?

In the case of the preacher, he *stirs up* opposition when he attempts to impress upon people the importance of devotional service. Śrīla Prabhupāda writes, "While engaged in preaching work, he has to meet with so many opposing elements, and therefore the *sādhu*, or devotee of the Lord, has to be very tolerant." (*Bhāg*. 3.25.21, purport)

Going against popular opinion is particularly difficult for children growing up in a Kṛṣṇa conscious environment. The devotee children are usually happy in early childhood as they worship Kṛṣṇa with their parents, but once they begin to mix with nondevotee peers, the pressure for conformity threatens their devotional life. One boy named Haridāsa became very unhappy as he began to associate with children at the local public school. He started to resent his odd Sanskrit name and the fact that he was a vegetarian, as well as many other things connected with devotional service. The situation became so tense that the parents decided to seek help from a psychologist who specialized in family counseling. The psychologist suggested to Haridāsa, who was ten years old, that it was not so bad to be different from other people. He pointed out that some of us *are* different, and we do not have to be ashamed of it. The positive suggestion worked, and Haridāsa took courage in accepting the fact that he was different from the average American boy. But many devotee children find it extremely difficult and will do anything they can not to be seen as strange. This problem presents itself as one of the great challenges to raising children in Kṛṣṇa consciousness.

At least adults should not be oversensitive to the fact that not everyone likes a Vaiṣṇava. When the Kṛṣṇa consciousness movement won its first anti-cult case in New York, *Time* reported it with the heading, "The Right To Be Strange." Whether we like it or not, devotees are considered strange in most Western countries, and it is something that should not trouble us.

Deep Convictions

A devotee is deeply convinced of Vedic teachings. If an ignorant person criticizes the life of devotional service, a devotee knows this is ignorance that is based on the bodily conception of life. He is not swayed. Mahārāja Rahūgaṇa insulted the great *brāhmaṇa* Jaḍa Bharata with many words of sarcasm, but Jaḍa Bharata smiled and spoke the following words:

> You have said that I am not stout and strong, and these words are befitting a person who does not know the distinction between the body and the soul. The body may be fat or thin, but no learned man would say such things of the spirit soul. As far as the spirit soul is concerned, I am neither fat nor skinny; therefore you are correct when you say that I am not very stout. Also, if the object of this journey and the path leading there were mine, there would be many troubles for me, but because they relate not to me but to my body, there is no trouble at all.
>
> As far as your thinking that you are the king and master and thus trying to order me, this is also incorrect because these positions are temporary. Today you are a king and I am your servant, but tomorrow the position may be changed, and you may be my servant and I your master.
>
> My dear king, you have said, "You rascal, you dull, crazy fellow! I am going to chastise you, and then you will come to your senses." In this regard, let me say that although I live like a dull, deaf and dumb man, I am actually a self-realized person. What will you gain by punishing me?
>
> —*Bhāg.* 5.10.9,11,13

I shaved my head as a devotee in 1966 because I thought it would please Śrīla Prabhupāda. But when I went out into the streets of the Lower East Side and a few people hooted at me, I was surprised and hurt. The ridicule felt like a push from behind. And yet it made me conscious of Kṛṣṇa and Prabhupāda; I had lost my anonymity! When I went back to the storefront and presented myself before Śrīla Prabhupāda, he said, "Thank you very much." During the same year Śrīla Prabhupāda gave us *japa* beads, he said that we should always carry them with us, "If you're not ashamed." We should not be ashamed that we are followers of Lord Kṛṣṇa who wear Vaiṣṇava *tilaka*. A few people may think we are crazy, but many others will ask us out of curiosity, "What is the marking on your forehead? Is this some kind of religion?" Such questions are glorious because they are about Kṛṣṇa and therefore they are of benefit to the whole world.

Osmosis

Because devotees live in the world, they sometimes feel influenced by it. This happens by a process of osmosis, whereby one gradually, and often unconsciously, assimilates his environment. As you breathe in the atmosphere of the non-devotees, it is likely that you will become somewhat like them. Devotees begin following the latest trends in electronic appliances, clothing fashions, and street slang. It is not necessarily wrong to be aware of the latest "state-of-the-art" computers, because such things can be used in the service of Kṛṣṇa. But it may be that a devotee becomes motivated by desires other than pure service. We are not immune to the psychological influence of advertising and political propaganda that affects everyone else in society. Businessmen see devotees as just another type of customer, even if dressed a little strangely. And so devotees become sucked into the same traps as everyone else, because we live in the world. From the viewpoint of pure devotional service, these are obstacles on the path.

In order to protect the devotees from being absorbed into the "pop" consciousness of mundane society, Śrīla Prabhupāda created a subculture. Included in the charter of the International Society for Krishna Consciousness, as written by Śrīla Prabhupāda, are several references to a society of devotees:

> (1) To bring the members of the Society together with each other and nearer to Krishna, the Prime Entity, thus to develop the idea within the members, and humanity at large, that each soul is part and parcel of the quality of Godhead (Krishna).
> (2) To erect for the members and for society at large, a holy place of transcendental pastimes, dedicated to the Personality of Krishna.
> (3) To bring the members closer together for the purpose of teaching a simpler and more natural way of life.

The Kṛṣṇa conscious society lives within the buildings of ISKCON. The society is also found in the congregation of devotees who live in their own homes, but who sometimes gather together in the temple or in each other's homes for the purpose of sharing Kṛṣṇa consciousness. Devotees are social beings, and so the obstacle of being too influenced by the mundane world can only be surmounted by living in the society of like-minded friends.

When Do We Compromise?

"Being different" in every respect may be invigorating for some devotees, but not all. Prabhupāda said that there were many *realistic* obstacles. This means that sometimes we have to compromise. We cannot demand of ourselves or of other devotees that we always act with the utmost aggression against the opposing forces of materialism. We also have to learn to live in peace alongside the nondevotees.

Some devotees feel it is too heavy and too demanding for them to wear Vaiṣṇava dress in public. Those who always wear *dhotis* or *saris* should not preach that unless one appears in public in devotee dress, with shaved head or *sarī*, etc., then one is in *māyā*. Better to speak in a positive way of the good effect of Vaiṣṇava dress—that people who see us will think Hare Kṛṣṇa and gain in spiritual benefit—but if a devotee is too shy to do it, we should not make him feel guilty or bad. *Gṛhasthas* especially have to integrate more with the ordinary society and maintain an identity as "normal" persons. We ought to encourage each other not to be overwhelmed by the nondevotee world, to maintain our chanting, hearing and serving, but this has to be done according to individual capacity.

Somehow or other we have to preserve our integrity as Vaiṣṇavas. The devotees are like ambassadors from the spiritual world who represent Kṛṣṇa in a foreign country of the earth. Yet even ambassadors have to blend in certain ways within the foreign culture in which they are living. A devotee has to pay his bills like everyone else, and it is not forbidden for a devotee to vote in local or national elections. We are forced to participate in national emergencies. But in most cases there is a Kṛṣṇa conscious way to respond to these various cultural demands.

People are also curious to see how the devotee acts in the world. Prabhupāda was pleased when some of his devotees in Australia rescued people from a burning office building. We take it as good publicity when devotees do something which is commendable even to the nondevotees, and there is certainly nothing wrong with getting some good "P.Ṛ." for Kṛṣṇa's cause. Only when the devotees are actually adored can there be peace in the world:

> When will that day come when a temple will be established in every house in every corner of the world?
>
> When will the high court judge be a Gauḍīya Vaiṣṇava with tilaka beautifully decorating his forehead?
>
> When will a Vaiṣṇava winning votes be elected president of the land and preaching be spread everywhere?
>
> —Śrīla Prabhupāda's Vyāsa-pūjā homage of 1961, quoted in *Śrīla Prabhupāda-līlāmṛta*, Vol 1, p. 250

A devotee does not hate the world or see it as false. He sees it as Kṛṣṇa's energy. The *Īśopaniṣad* mantra states, "One who always sees all living entities as spiritual sparks, in quality one with the Lord, becomes a true knower of things. What, then, can be illusion or anxiety for him?" (*Śrī Īśopaniṣad*, Mantra 7)

A devotee is confident that he has a right to perform his duties in the world, as much as any nondevotee does. In Vedic culture *sādhus* were given free access wherever they went because people knew that they should be respected and received as messengers of the Supreme Lord. Śrīla Prabhupāda used to chide the attitude of immigration officials who questioned him as he entered countries on his preaching mission. Prabhupāda reasoned, "They call the country Australia, but it is actually Kṛṣṇa's country. A devotee sees every place as belonging to Kṛṣṇa, and so he should be allowed to go freely and speak there."

If we exaggerate our opposition to the world, then we will fall prey to the definitions given of dangerous cults. According to sociologists, one characteristic of an undesirable cult is that the members feel strong paranoia toward the rest of the world. This was one of the main insanities of the Jim Jones cult; they thought the outside world was coming to attack them, and so the cult members committed group suicide. The devotee of Kṛṣṇa does not hate or fear the world. He preserves his integrity, keeps a respectful distance toward the sinful ways of his brothers and sisters, and yet he is part of human society and feels compassion for everyone.

As Prabhupāda noted in his ISKCON charter, the society was to develop Kṛṣṇa consciousness "within the members *and humanity at large*." The temple was to be erected not just for the members but for "society at large." This is the preaching spirit expressed by Prahlāda Mahārāja to Lord Nṛsiṁhadeva: "I do not wish to be liberated alone, leaving aside all these poor fools and rascals. I know that without Kṛṣṇa consciousness, without taking shelter of Your lotus feet, one cannot be happy. Therefore I wish to bring them back to shelter at Your lotus feet." (*Bhāg.* 7.9.44)

A Vaiṣṇava is friendly to all and seeks the welfare of the nondevotees, yet for his intimate association he prefers to be with the devotees of the Lord. Lord Caitanya defined a Vaiṣṇava as one who renounces the association of sense enjoyers. Narottama dāsa Ṭhākura said that he wished to be with those persons, either householders or *sannyāsīs*, who sincerely cried out, "Ah, Gaurāṅga!" Devotees are naturally attracted to the soothing *saṅga* of those with whom they can sing *bhajanas* of Kṛṣṇa and talk about Kṛṣṇa. Materialists are interested in money and sense gratification, but devotees want to please Kṛṣṇa. Whenever we find persons who are interested in hearing about Kṛṣṇa, we prefer their company. And we avoid the association of *asat* or demoniac persons. It is therefore definitely a strain and an obstacle for a devotee when he or she has to work with *asat* persons or live intimately with them.

Money Problems

The problem of maintaining Kṛṣṇa consciousness while raising money is common both to the temple devotees and to those living outside. Methods of fund-raising to maintain temples sometimes come into conflict with the devotee's desire for a peaceful life of chanting and hearing. It is beyond the scope of this book to discuss how the temples of ISKCON should finance themselves. But I will discuss obstacles met by *gṛhasthas* who work with nondevotees, and some of these obstacles will also be applicable to temple devotees.

Nārada Muni and Prabhupāda, in the Seventh Canto of *Śrīmad-Bhāgavatam*, give relevant instructions for how *gṛhasthas* may earn their livelihood without sacrificing Kṛṣṇa consciousness. There is no indication that by earning money one is dishonored or considered a "*karmī*" or less of a devotee. Rather, Lord Kṛṣṇa criticizes the false transcendentalist who refuses to work and lives at the expense of honest *gṛhasthas*:

> On the other hand, if a sincere person tries to control the active senses by the mind and begins karma-yoga (in Kṛṣṇa consciousness) without attachment, he is by far superior.
>
> Purport
>
> Instead of becoming a pseudo transcendentalist for the sake of wanton living and sense enjoyment, it is far better to remain in one's own business and execute the purpose of life, which is to get free from material bondage and enter into the kingdom of God. . . . A householder can also reach this destination by regulated service in Kṛṣṇa consciousness. . . . A sincere person who follows this method is far better situated than the false pretender who adopts show-bottle spiritualism to cheat the innocent public. A sincere sweeper in the street is far better than a charlatan meditator who meditates only for the sake of making a living.
>
> —Bg. 3.7

In the Eighteenth Chapter of *Bhagavad-gītā*, "The Perfection of Renunciation," Lord Kṛṣṇa gives His opinion that one should not give up prescribed duties. Prabhupāda writes, "One who is in Kṛṣṇa consciousness should not give up earning money out of fear that he is performing fruitive activities. If by working one can engage his money in Kṛṣṇa consciousness. . . one should not desist out of fear or because such activities are considered troublesome." (Bg. 18.8, purport) Prabhupāda goes on to praise "many members of the International Society for Kṛṣṇa Consciousness who work very hard in their office or factory," and calls them "actually *sannyāsīs*" because they give from their earnings for the purpose of Kṛṣṇa consciousness.

Nārada's Advice to Gṛhasthas

In Nārada Muni's instructions to Yudhiṣṭhira, a *gṛhastha* is advised to associate with saintly persons and hear about Kṛṣṇa. He should not claim that these activities have to be given up because of daily work.

> One should work eight hours at the most to earn his livelihood, and either in the afternoon or in the evening, a householder should associate with devotees to hear about the incarnations of Kṛṣṇa and His activities and thus be gradually liberated from the clutches of *māyā*. However, instead of finding time to hear about Kṛṣṇa, the householders, after working hard in offices and factories, find time to go to a restaurant or a club where instead of hearing about Kṛṣṇa and His activities they are very much pleased to hear about the political activities of demons and nondevotees and to enjoy sex life, wine, women and meat and in this way waste their time. This is not *gṛhastha* life, but demoniac life.
>
> —*Bhāg*. 7.14.4, purport

Nārada advises that one should earn his livelihood "as much as necessary to maintain body and soul together," and continue a detached attitude while living in human society. Prabhupāda comments:

> A wise man . . . concludes that in the human form of life he should not endeavor for unnecessary necessities, but should live a very simple life, just maintaining body and soul together. Certainly one requires some means of livelihood, and according to one's *varṇa* and *āśrama* this means of livelihood is prescribed in the *śāstras*. One should be satisfied with this. Therefore, instead of hankering for more and more money, a sincere devotee of the Lord tries to invent some ways to earn his livelihood, and when he does so Kṛṣṇa helps him.
>
> —*Bhāg*. 7.14.5, purport

Nārada also advises one not to be a thief and claim proprietorship of all his wealth, but spend extra money for advancing oneself in Kṛṣṇa consciousness.

> The *gṛhasthas* should give contributions for constructing temples to the Supreme Lord and for preaching of *Śrīmad-Bhagavad-gītā*, or Kṛṣṇa consciousness, all over the world. . . . The Kṛṣṇa consciousness movement therefore affords one such an opportunity to spend his extra earnings for the benefit of all human society by expanding Kṛṣṇa consciousness. In India especially we see hundreds and thousands of temples that were constructed by the wealthy men of society who did not want to be called thieves and be punished.
>
> —*Bhāg*. 7.14.8, purport

Nārada advises King Yudhiṣṭhira and all *gṛhasthas* to avoid *ugrākarma*, work which is hellishly difficult, risky, and implicated with sin. Prabhupāda comments:

> Men are engaging in many sinful activities and becoming degraded by opening slaughterhouses, breweries and cigarette factories, as well as nightclubs and other establishments for sense enjoyment. In this way they are spoiling their lives. In all of these activities, of course, householders are involved, and therefore it is advised here, with the use of the word *api*, that even though one is a householder, one should not engage himself in severe hardships. One's means of livelihood should be extremely simple.
>
> —*Bhāg*. 7.14.10, purport

Those devotees who donate their money for spreading Kṛṣṇa consciousness are as meritorious as the devotees who actually spend the money in preaching activities. If a worker is hesitant to hand over his hard-earned money to the local temple, he can spend with his own hand for a worthy Kṛṣṇa conscious project or a project which he directs himself. One can buy Prabhupāda's books and distribute them or send money to foreign missions of Kṛṣṇa consciousness. Spending money for the spiritual development of one's own family members, by setting up Deity worship in the home, or by taking one's family on pilgrimage to the holy *dhāmas* in India are all good ways to spiritualize earnings and to purify the sacrifice of work. As Lord Kṛṣṇa states, "Work done as a sacrifice for Viṣṇu has to be performed, otherwise work causes bondage in this material world." (*Bg*. 3.9)

By using money in Kṛṣṇa consciousness, the worker is not only freed from bad effects of *karma*, but he derives personal satisfaction which makes the austerities of labor more meaningful. A householder's charity should be given by him freely and out of his own sense of duty. Prabhupāda writes, "Charity is sometimes performed for elevation to the heavenly kingdom and sometimes with great trouble and with repentance afterwards: 'Why have I spent so much in this way?' Charity is also sometimes given under some obligation, at the request of a superior. These kinds of charity are said to be given in the mode of passion." (Bg. 17.21, purport)

Thinking of Kṛṣṇa While Working

Lord Kṛṣṇa advises that His devotees should "always think of Me," but this may prove particularly difficult for a *gṛhastha* at his work place. Externally, his work may have nothing to do with Kṛṣṇa. It is relatively easy to see the connection between work and devotion if you are dressing the Deity on the altar, or cleaning the temple floor, but what if your work is to repair cars or computers? Śrīla Prabhupāda advises us to select our method of work in consultation with the spiritual master and not do something whimsically. But when one is convinced that his work is authorized devotional service, then he can engage in a moment-to-moment meditation even while at his place of work.

> And while working in that way, one should think of Kṛṣṇa only: 'I have been appointed to discharge this particular duty by Kṛṣṇa.' While acting in such a way, one naturally has to think of Kṛṣṇa. This is perfect Kṛṣṇa consciousness.
>
> —Bg. 18.57, purport

Aside from meditating on one's purpose, one can also chant Hare Kṛṣṇa always, either aloud or chanting within the mind. Although a worker in a mundane establishment might seem to be at a disadvantage compared to a temple chanter, it is sometimes even more meaningful to call on the names of the Lord in a difficult situation than in the relaxed atmosphere of the temple routine. At any rate, the *gṛhastha* does not have the luxury of staying home to chant, so he must learn to adapt himself in the so-called material situation. Lord Kṛṣṇa expected Arjuna to remain in Kṛṣṇa consciousness even on a battlefield.

> He [Kṛṣṇa] does not advise Arjuna simply to remember Him and give up his occupation. No, the Lord never suggests anything impractical. In this material world, in order to maintain the body one has to work. . . . The Lord therefore tells Arjuna that he need not give up his occupation, but while he is engaged in his occupation he should remember Kṛṣṇa *(mām anusmara)*. If he doesn't practice remembering Kṛṣṇa while he is struggling for existence, then it will not be possible for him to remember Kṛṣṇa at the time of death.
>
> —*Bhagavad-gītā As It Is*, Introduction

Making Friends

Gṛhasthas sometimes ask if it is all right to develop friendly relationships with workers who are not Kṛṣṇa conscious devotees. The answer should be "Yes." Even if it is not possible to speak directly about Kṛṣṇa to a fellow worker, one can at least set a good example by being friendly and conscientious on the job. This indirect method of representing Kṛṣṇa is often more effective in making a good impression than showy religious displays. There is a limit, however, in how freely a devotee will want to mix with those who have no interest in Kṛṣṇa consciousness or in following religious principles. Perhaps you cannot be the hit of the office party because you do not drink liquor, smoke, or chase after women. If refraining from licentious behavior means that one does not become intimate with the boss, then that is the price one has to pay. But gradually, fellow workers will see the devotee as a person of reliable character, and they will admire him, even if they do not practice the higher principles themselves. A supervisor of a counseling agency regularly turned to the Kṛṣṇa devotee among his counselors whenever difficult cases arose. He said, "You have a special peacefulness within you. You can deal with these cases."

Alternative Occupations

Although I cannot presume to give advice to *gṛhasthas* as to what type of work they should take, I may at least mention that one should consider various alternatives. One should not think his only choices are to get into the insurance business or the computer business. One alternative for solving the economic problems is that which is given in the *Vedas:* an economy based on cow protection and land development. This has proven to be very difficult for Western devotees to take up. Many of the spiritual farm communities are actually supported by urban business enterprises such as painting sales. But there are pioneers in different parts of the world who are trying their best to raise money on the basis of self-sufficiency. When one is deciding on a career, he owes it to himself to at least look into what some of these pioneers are doing. For example, at the Śaraṇāgati Farm in British Columbia, devotees build their own simple homes and live without electricity or phones. Some of them grow gardens and produce enough canned vegetables for a whole winter's supply without purchasing from the market.

Another alternative is to engage in full-time Kṛṣṇa conscious preaching. To cite an example, Apūrva Prabhu and his wife Kamalinī run a small vegetarian restaurant in Lansing, Michigan, where they also sell Prabhupāda's books. They manage to support themselves and their children by this enterprise. Kṛṣṇa helps them and they make their maintenance money while engaged as full-time preachers. This does not mean that those who work at other trades are "in *māyā*." Kṛṣṇa will be most pleased according to a devotee's sincerity, which may be displayed in many different work situations. But before choosing a means of livelihood, a devotee ought to consider all the instructions given by *Śrīmad-Bhāgavatam* and Śrīla Prabhupāda. Try to find something which does not make you miserable and perform it as a sacrifice for pleasing Lord Kṛṣṇa. Prabhupāda refers to this as the "great art of doing work," and he indicates that any labor undertaken not for sense gratification but for the satisfaction of Kṛṣṇa will bring the right result. "This practice will not only save one from the reaction of work, but also gradually elevate one to transcendental loving service of the Lord, which alone can raise one to the kingdom of God." (Bg. 3.9, purport)

Obstacles Caused by the Mind

Lord Kṛṣṇa says, "For him who has conquered the mind, the mind is the best of friends; but for one who has failed to do so, his mind will remain the greatest enemy." (Bg. 6.6) The mind is part of the subtle body, consisting of mind, intelligence, and false ego. Mind is the center of sensory activities. Śrīla Prabhupāda writes, "Mind is the center of all the activities of the senses, and thus when we hear about sense objects the mind generally becomes a reservoir of all ideas of sense gratification; and as a result, the mind and the senses become the repository of lust." (Bg. 3.40, purport)

All transcendentalists seek to control the mind, rather than being controlled by the mind. In many cases it is the mind alone which makes the obstacles on the path seem insurmountable.

Therefore, by controlling the mind we can solve many of the problems we have been discussing: doubts in Kṛṣṇa consciousness, illicit sex, inability to chant, and so on.

There is valuable information about the mind in the Eleventh Canto of *Śrīmad-Bhāgavatam*, in the chapter called "The Song of the Avanti *brāhmaṇa*." The Avanti *brāhmaṇa* was a rich businessman who was prone to anger and cruelty. By the will of providence and by *karma*, he lost all his money. Then he took to renunciation. But when he sat to meditate, people would tease him and abuse him. Enduring all insults, he sang a song about detachment:

> . . . These people are not the cause of my happiness and distress. Neither are the demigods, my own body, the planets, my past work, or time. Rather, it is the mind alone that causes happiness and distress and perpetuates the rotation of material life.
>
> —*Bhāg*. 11.23.42

> All the senses have been under the control of the mind since time immemorial, and the mind himself never comes under the sway of any other. He is stronger than the strongest, and his godlike power is fearsome. Therefore, anyone who can bring the mind under control becomes the master of all the senses.
>
> Failing to conquer this irrepressible enemy, the mind, whose urges are intolerable and who torments the heart, many people are completely bewildered and create useless quarrel with others. Thus they conclude that other people are either their friends, enemies or indifferent to them.
>
> —*Bhāg*. 11.23.47–48

The Avanti *brāhmaṇa* concluded that he should take shelter of the lotus feet of Kṛṣṇa and thus solve all his problems. Seen from the viewpoint of the Absolute, our problems are imaginary. That is, they are mostly *in the mind*. Take, for example, physical illness. When you are sick, you may become depressed and even lose your faith in God, who "made this happen to me." But when you control your mind, you accept your illness and deepen your relationship with Kṛṣṇa. Physical disease is not imaginary, but whether we see it favorably or unfavorably depends upon the position of the mind.

Real mental control is achieved by fixing the mind in service to Kṛṣṇa. A person who is situated in self-realization meets obstacles on the path by dealing with them in a practical, philosophical way, and remains fixed in Kṛṣṇa consciousness. But persons whose minds are weak find even small-sized problems very troublesome. Therefore, we say that their real problem is the mind itself.

An important breakthrough for persons who are dominated by their minds comes when they are able to see themselves as different than the mind. If I am entirely dominated by my own mind, then I cannot detach myself from its "reality." I described this experience in a stanza of a poem:

This subtle mind-stuff!
You cannot see it jump,
it does not have a color,
it's not reflected in the water,
but it seems more real
than the five great elements.
When I go out to walk
it goes with me,
struggling through the mud.

An uncontrolled mind becomes especially destructive when it turns in the direction of illicit sex. Once the mind (the center of sensory activities) becomes obsessed with the desire to perform masturbation or sexual intercourse with another person, *then* there is little a person can do but become a slave to the compulsion. Our only hope is to catch hold of reality before the fearsome mind seizes onto its own version. Śrīla Prabhupāda has described three psychic functions, thinking, feeling and willing. As far as possible, we have to become aware of the mind's actions in the thinking stage, and use our intelligence to overcome the mind. Then right thinking will be followed by right feeling and acting. According to Rūpa Gosvāmī's *Upadeśāmṛta*, only one who can control the pushing agent of the mind as well as the tongue, belly, and genitals can be considered a *gosvāmī* or controller of the senses.

Tactics: The Broom and the Shoe

The Vaiṣṇava *ācāryas* offer various tactics to help us in controlling the wayward mind so that we may place it in service of the higher self. One technique is to ignore the mind. Viśvanātha Cakravartī states that this can be done by making prior vows or fixing our determination for Kṛṣṇa consciousness. He gives the example of a vow a devotee takes for fasting on *Janmāṣṭami* day. During the day, hunger will come, and the mind will demand food. But because the intelligence has become fixed in its decision for fasting, one can ignore the mind's clamoring voice.

Another tactic offered by Bhaktisiddhānta Sarasvatī Ṭhākura is that "as soon as you wake in the morning you should beat your mind a hundred times with a broom and at night before taking rest beat it another hundred times with a shoe." When this example is spoken, it usually draws smiles. But it is a serious proposal. Does it mean that we should actually strike our head with a stiff broom? Yes, it can be obeyed in that literal way. It also means figuratively beating some sense into yourself. As soon as we wake, our mind is filled with dictations based on the desires of the senses. But rather than submissively obeying these proposals, which are often nonsensical, we should take hold of the mind and "beat it" by intelligent decision-making, followed by determined action.

For example, when I wake in the morning and look at my clock, I may see that it is time to rise for attending *maṅgala-ārati*. But my mind may say, "No, I want to stay in bed. It's too cold to get up." This proposal is unacceptable to my real purpose, so I have to reject it. Bhaktisiddhānta Sarasvatī Ṭhākura's recommendation of "a hundred times" implies that there is not only one silly or destructive idea but many of them. They need to be beaten while they are in the formulative stage. And so he has told us to reach for the broom. If the advice sounds humorous, that is good. Unless we are able to laugh at ourselves, we may end up taking the mind's demands too seriously. No, I am not my mind. I am pure spirit soul, eternal servant of Kṛṣṇa.

The beating proposed here is not a masochistic act. The negating of foolish demands is accompanied by positive instructions from *guru*, *śāstra*, and *sādhu*. But we have to first show the mind who's boss, or else we will follow the way of the fickle *(cañcala)* mind.

Easing on the Reins

Sometimes it is best to make peace with the mind. If we give the mind only harsh blows and restraint, it will find a way to revolt. As in horse riding, one has to pull the reins tightly, but if one does that constantly and too tightly, the horse will buck. We have to let the horse know who is in charge, but sometimes we have to give him a little lead and let him run. Say we are trying to control the mind from the compulsion of overeating. We know that overeating is an obstacle on the path of devotional service. But does that mean we shall force the mind to not even think of food or that we should starve our body? The tongue makes a demand to the mind for something palatable, and so we concede, "Yes you may eat, but eat only Kṛṣṇa *prasādam*, and not too much." By a combination of predetermined decisions as to what we shall eat, as well as ignoring the mind's extravagant demands, along with a rational explanation about the after-effects of overeating, we can avoid overeating without "killing" the mind. After all, Kṛṣṇa does not say that the mind is always the enemy, but that it can become a well-wishing friend.

The compromises we allow the mind should be within the rules and regulations of devotional service. Our aspiration is for devotional service to Kṛṣṇa—not sense gratification. In the beginning stages this is achieved by following "the regulated principles of freedom," in the form of various rules and regulations. In the highest stage, the devotee enters a devotional trance, *samādhi*, and desires nothing but loving service to Lord Kṛṣṇa.

Moment to Moment

We may be able to reach a general condition of sanity by which we control our mind from telling us to commit sinful and deviant acts. And yet we find ourselves unable to control the mind on a minute-to-minute basis. We are able to control ourselves so that we desire to spend the day in devotional service, without serious doubts about the philosophy and without schemes for illicit sex. In that sense we have a resolved intelligence. But from moment to moment we remain distracted. When we chant *japa*, we cannot concentrate on the sound of the mantra. When we go before the Deity for *darśana*, our eyes see the divine form, but our mind drags us all over the universe. By the time *darśana* is over, we realize that we have not been able to concentrate at all on the lotus feet of the Lord. This is an unfortunate stage in which a devotee may go through bona fide activities one after another in a mechanical way, without absorption in devotional service.

Devotees sometimes complain that they find the morning program, which consists mostly of singing Sanskrit *ślokas*, to be boring. One way to engage the mind during these activities is to be more aware of the meaning of the *bhajanas*. This will help us in chanting the *mahā-mantra*, and also in viewing the Deity. For example, at *maṅgala-ārati*, devotees sing "*Gurvāṣṭaka*," which consists of praises to the spiritual master. This *bhajana* creates a very specific mood of worship. Each verse tells how the guru guides the disciples—in *kīrtana*, Deity worship, offering of *prasādam*, and so on. After singing "*Gurvāṣṭaka*," we sing the prayers to Nṛsiṁhadeva, which are quite different from the prayers to the spiritual master. We ask the half-lion, half-man incarnation of the Lord for protection against the demons. Immediately after that we sing an astounding *bhajana* to the *tulasī* plant. In this song we seek to become assistants of the *gopīs* in the *līlā* of Rādhā and Kṛṣṇa in Goloka. If we say each of these prayers as if they are all in the same mood, this is because we do not pay attention to the words. But if we become familiar with the translations, then even if we cannot think in terms of Sanskrit grammar, the meaning of the words will strike at us. If we focus on the meaning of *śrī-rādhā-govinda-preme sadā jena bhāsi*, and think of Rādhā and Govinda and of being Their servants—and if we feel when we sing *mahāprabhoḥ kīrtana-nṛtya-gīta*, which tells of the guru's ecstasy in leading us in *harināma*—and if we think of the next verse, *śrī-vigrahārā* . . . which describes how the spiritual master leads us in worshiping the Deity—then we will find ourselves engaged in transcendental meditation on many sublime aspects of devotional life. By thinking of the words as we recite them, we will feel more enlivened and not be bored. This is a good tactic for training the mind, which, when left to its own devices, becomes stronger and stronger in rascaldom.

"My Dear Mind"

As with other obstacles, the Vaiṣṇava *ācāryas* are aware of the obstacles presented by the wayward mind. They have expressed this struggle in "Prayers to the Mind." Some of the favorites are *Bhajahū Re Mana* by Govinda dāsa, *Manaḥ Śikṣā* by Ragunātha dāsa Gosvāmī, and Bhaktisiddhānta Sarasvatī Ṭhākura's prayers to his mind. Bhaktisiddhānta Sarasvatī Ṭhākura prays, "Oh my mind, why aren't you a Vaiṣṇava?" Each of these verses can be studied carefully, and they will help us to better understand the dilemma of the uncontrolled mind.

In their songs to the mind, the *ācāryas* recognize that the mind is different from the real self. They often identify the mind as being a non-Vaiṣṇava. The devotee enters into a dialogue with the mind and makes strong appeals in favor of Kṛṣṇa consciousness. The intelligence or soul speaks to this uncontrollable person, the mind. The higher self does not have complete control of the situation, but he makes his appeal, "My dear mind, please be a Vaiṣṇava. Why are you lusting after women? You should know that all women belong to Kṛṣṇa." And Bhaktisiddhānta Sarasvatī Ṭhākura asks, "My dear mind, why are you lusting after fame? Do you not know it's not better than the dung of a boar?"

Let us not describe our friend the mind only in a negative way. Sometimes when we rise early we are in a peaceful state, and we begin to chant *japa* with the cooperation of our friend. The scriptures give the analogy of the chariot driver and the horses. The driver is compared to the intelligence, and the reins are compared to the mind. When we chant in good consciousness, we can feel the pull of the reins (the mind), but we maintain control. When a driver is conducting powerful horses, he is not angry with them or fighting against them, but he enjoys the control and also the pull of the horses. When the horses are running quickly, under control, it is an exciting cooperation. When we chant nicely, we will find that with a slight effort we send messages to the mind, "You're doing very nicely; please continue hearing the holy names." But we remain vigilant, and as soon as the mind veers a little to the left, we tug it back onto the main road. We warn our friend, "Do not go after sense gratification." And neither do we completely ignore the mind. If the mind repeatedly says, "But it's too hot in here, it's too hot for chanting," we may reply, "All right my friend, I'll open the window. But you just go on chanting Hare Kṛṣṇa Hare Kṛṣṇa Kṛṣṇa Kṛṣṇa Hare Hare, Hare Rāma Hare Rāma Rāma Rāma Hare Hare." When the mind finally submits to chanting the Lord's names, then mind, body, intelligence, and soul all enjoy a *samādhi* of transcendental loving service. In this state of intimate union with Lord Kṛṣṇa, we can easily deal with any obstacles that appear on the road.

The Fighting Spirit

As long as we are in the material world, there will always be one kind of obstacle or another. When we fully surrender to Kṛṣṇa, however, then all the obstacles will become sources of happiness. As Bhaktivinoda Ṭhākura says, "I consider the troubles which I encounter while engaged in your service to be a source of happiness."

Lord Gopāla's pure devotee, Mādhavendra Purī, undertook great difficulty in order to collect sandalwood at the request of his Deity. Mādhavendra Purī risked his life at the hands of thieves on the road, and he had to face innumerable watchmen and toll collectors. He walked for thousands of miles. But he undertook all these hardships with a feeling of love because he was doing it as service to Kṛṣṇa. Although we cannot imitate Mādhavendra Purī, we should look for a spirit of personal enjoyment while engaged in the struggle to serve Kṛṣṇa. We all seek pleasure, and since we have to face problems, we might as well enjoy the struggle for Kṛṣṇa.

The opposite mentality of this is to always seek the complacent way, to be ease-loving. But easy-going life and Kṛṣṇa consciousness do not go well together.

Kṣatriyas in Spirit

The best example of those who enjoy a good fight are the *kṣatriyas*. When Mahārāja Parīkṣit learned that the symptoms of the Age of Quarrel had begun to infiltrate within his state, "he did not think the matter very palatable. This did, however, give him a chance to fight." (*Bhāg*. 1.16.10) Śrīla Prabhupāda writes, "A perfect *kṣatriya* king is always jubilant as soon as he gets a chance to fight, just as a sportsman is eager when there is a chance for a sporting match." (*Bhāg*. 1.16.10, purport) Similarly, when Dhṛtarāṣṭra, on the advice of Vidura, left his comfortable home and went to practice austerities, he looked forward to the risks that awaited him:

> The gentle and chaste Gāndhārī, who was the daughter of King Subala of Kandahar [or Gāndhāra], followed her husband, seeing that he was going to the Himalaya Mountains, which are the delight of those who have accepted the staff of the renounced order like fighters who have accepted a good lashing from the enemy.
>
> —*Bhāg*. 1.13.30

We may not be physically fit or bold enough to fight like a *kṣatriya*, but we can become *kṣatriya*-like in spirit. This will be required if we are going to do battle with staunch opponents like our own mind.

A healthy organism thrives on a certain amount of stress by which he exercises his will to live. Although psychologists often tell us how to reduce stress in the modern age, we also have to learn how to live with stress. The body is made strong by stress and tension. When properly applied, tension creates art, music, and athletic prowess. When a healthy human being exerts himself or herself in the cause of Kṛṣṇa, that is called *tapasya*, stress for a good purpose.

A Series of Problems

Recently while I was traveling in Eastern Europe, I encountered many problems on the road. First we had engine trouble, then the petrol stations went on strike, then we had to obtain the required visas. When we reached Prague, we could not find a telephone, and after we found one, we discovered that there was no one at home at the Hare Kṛṣṇa center. We waited all day in the street to see if devotees would show up at their address. When they finally arrived, I felt great relief. It seemed that all our obstacles were now removed. The devotees invited us to come with them to their farm—but then another problem arose: would our van be able to make it over the rough country roads? At this point I realized that I should stop looking for the cessation to problems but be prepared to meet them one after another. And so I wrote in my diary:

> Life is a series of problems executed on behalf of Lord Kṛṣṇa and Prabhupāda, with nectar rest periods in between. Since our objective is to please Kṛṣṇa, we will show our sincerity by being willing to work to overcome the problems.

Problem-solving in Bhakti-yoga

In devotional service the real goal of problem-solving is to please Kṛṣṇa by your endeavors. If you execute duties successfully but do not succeed in pleasing Kṛṣṇa, then what is the benefit? An expert *karmī* who claims he never has money problems and who has a healthy, aggressive mentality may think that he is an expert "trouble-shooter." And yet a simple Vaiṣṇava, who may not have solved the problems of his material existence so well, is actually better at problem-solving because he always depends on Kṛṣṇa. Kṛṣṇa promises, "My devotee will never be vanquished."

A devotee does not think of obstacles that come to him as his own problems. He leaves the results up to Kṛṣṇa, so if anything goes wrong, it is Kṛṣṇa's problem, not the devotee's. The devotee is simply dedicated to always serving the Lord, whether in happiness or distress. Every day he faces whatever problems come his way and tries to solve them as part of his devotional service. They either get solved or not, but he does not mind, since his mission is to fully engage himself in *bhakti-yoga*.

The devotee's mentality is quite different from the materialist's. If the *karmī* does not solve his problem, then he is in anxiety. For example, if a devotee has to pay rent for the temple, he makes all endeavors but leaves the result up Kṛṣṇa. If he fails and has to leave the temple, he finds another place to serve and preach. He does not have to carry an undue burden of success or failure based on external events. In this way he is always successful, and there are ultimately no obstacles in the way of such a sincere servant. Even death is another opportunity to surrender to Kṛṣṇa.

So a devotee should never become hopeless. Lord Caitanya, speaking in the mood of the *gopīs*, declared, "Even if You handle me roughly in Your embrace or make me broken-hearted by not being present before me, You remain my worshipful Lord unconditionally." This surrendered attitude may also be applied to the chanting of a practicing devotee. Even if Kṛṣṇa does not appear to us in His holy name, and we cannot seem to overcome our offenses, still we will go on chanting. By surrendering to Kṛṣṇa, we become satisfied with the service itself. At least we do not become hopeless. We are thankful for the mercy of being able to always do some kind of service for Kṛṣṇa and guru. This surrendered attitude prevents one from becoming hopeless.

By facing problems, we also come to appreciate the nectar of victory when it actually comes. Kṛṣṇa mentions this as one of the reasons why He left the *gopīs* during the *rāsa* dance. He said, "If you think that I am too easily obtainable, you may take Me cheaply." Śrīla Prabhupāda gives the example of a person who loses money, searches for it frantically, and on finding it, becomes very happy and grateful. Spiritual life is a series of problems executed on behalf of Kṛṣṇa, with nectarean rest periods in between. When the difficulty is relieved by the bliss of victorious union with Kṛṣṇa, then it is nicer than anything we ever imagined.

Obstacles may also be seen as auspicious. Queen Kuntī said that dangers made her think more of Kṛṣṇa. And by thinking of Kṛṣṇa, she said, "We will no longer see repeated births and deaths." Therefore, she prayed that the calamities might continue so that she could think of Kṛṣṇa more. We are not as brave as Queen Kuntī, but whether we welcome troubles or not, they keep coming. Although we shudder when we see a formidable obstacle, we know that it is also good for us. We think, "This is what I wanted although it is a little painful; this will turn me more to Kṛṣṇa." Problems in life are not always solvable, but at least we can take a favorable attitude toward them, and then we will be successful. If we see the obstacles as all bad, we will miss the opportunity that accompanies them.

The concept of a fighting spirit will be more appealing to some than to others. Those with a pessimistic nature find it difficult to think their suffering is a cause of joy. Neither are they able to see their suffering as a service to Kṛṣṇa. The invitation to take obstacles in a chivalrous *kṣatriya*-like manner simply turns off persons of a pessimistic nature. If we cannot see the bright side of the problems in life, we should pray for strength to endure them. Pray to Kṛṣṇa to get us through. Prabhupāda writes, "There may be so many impediments for a person who is chanting Hare Kṛṣṇa. Nonetheless, tolerating all these impediments, one should continue to chant Hare Kṛṣṇa Hare Kṛṣṇa, Kṛṣṇa Kṛṣṇa Hare Hare/ Hare Rāma Hare Rāma, Rāma Rāma Hare Hare, so that at the end of one's life one can have the full benefit of Kṛṣṇa consciousness." (Bg. 8.5, purport)

A pure devotee does not like to ask Kṛṣṇa to remove the external calamities, but sometimes he does so by the force of circumstances. Gajendra called out to the Lord in helplessness when he was attacked by the crocodile, but he did it with regret.

At the very least, we should not make our sufferings a cause for losing faith in the Lord. We do not know Kṛṣṇa's inconceivable plan. We may think, "I have got enough problems, I am not going to welcome any more." In that case, we have to hold on to Kṛṣṇa's lotus feet, or to the feet of His pure devotee and think, "You're all I have to get me through. I find life to be nothing but troubles—which I *do not* welcome—but You're my savior, You're my one well-wisher, my light of hope in this dark life." If a person clings to Kṛṣṇa in that spirit, then he will become victorious.

Facing obstacles is a learning process. We may not feel happy about it, but we can note down in our book of experience, "This world is full of suffering; it is not a fit place for a gentlemen." Problems make us more serious about working for liberation. The world is not a happy place, so why be frivolous and waste time?

We have heard that in the heavenly planets life goes on without any wrinkles or anxieties—but finally ends in death. The people on higher planets often get so absorbed in their enjoyment that they forget they are the eternal servants of God. So obstacles on the path may serve to remind us of our higher destination. Unless we remember Kṛṣṇa, then the problems of life can turn into a degrading misery which makes us turn further away from Kṛṣṇa. And if we turn away from Lord Kṛṣṇa, we fall further and further into darkness.

If we find the problems of life bitter, we may also remember that happiness in the mode of goodness begins with poison and later becomes nectar. The obstacles are poisonous because they go against our plans for happiness. Everything seems ruined when things do not turn out the way we wanted them. But if we make service to Kṛṣṇa our main priority, then our unhappiness brings purification and promotion to Vaikuṇṭha, where there is no anxiety.

When Mahārāja Parīkṣit was cursed to die by a *brāhmaṇa* boy, he saw his frustration as a blessing from the Lord. By the curse he was able to disentangle himself from royal power and hear about Kṛṣṇa from Śukadeva Gosvāmī in the last seven days of his life. This assured his entrance to the spiritual world.

> The merciful Lord sometimes creates such awkward positions for His pure devotees in order to drag them towards Himself from the mire of material existence. But outwardly the situations appear to be frustrating to the devotees. The devotees of the Lord are always under the protection of the Lord, and in any condition, frustration or success, the Lord is the Supreme guide for the devotees. The pure devotees, therefore, accept all conditions of frustration as blessings from the Lord.
>
> —*Bhāg*. 1.18.28, purport

Glossary

A

ācārya—a spiritual master who teaches by example.

āśrama—the four spiritual orders of life: celibate student, householder, retired, and renounced life. Also, a dwelling place for spiritual shelter.

B

bhakti-yoga—linking with the Supreme Lord through devotional service.

brahmacārī—a celibate student.

brāhmaṇa—one wise in the *Vedas* who can guide others; the first Vedic social order.

D

daṇḍavats—literally, "falling down like a rod"; offering prostrated obeisances.

dhāma—abode, place of residence, usually referring to the Lord's abode.

G

gṛhastha—regulated householder life; the second order of Vedic spiritual life.

J

japa—soft, private chanting of the holy names.

K

Kali-yuga—The Age of Kali; the present age, characterized by quarrel; it is the last in the cycle of four ages and began five thousand years ago.

karma—fruitive action, for which there is always reaction, good or bad.

kīrtana—chanting the glories of the Supreme Lord.

M

mantra—a sound vibration that can deliver the mind from illusion.

māyā—(*mā*-not; *yā*-this), illusion; forgetfulness of one's relationship with Kṛṣṇa.

R

Rūpa Gosvāmī—the leader of the Six Gosvāmīs of Vṛndāvana, the principle followers of Lord Caitanya.

S

sādhana—regulated spiritual practices.

sannyāsī—a person in the renounced order of life, the fourth spiritual order in Vedic society.

śāstra—revealed scripture.

V

Vṛndāvana—the transcendental abode of Lord Kṛṣṇa.

Acknowledgements

I would like to thank the following disciples and friends who helped produce and print this book:

Ācārya dāsa
Ambikā-devī dāsī
Baladeva Vidyābhūṣaṇa dāsa
Bhagavan Ṛṣabha dāsa
Bhakta William Webb
Dattatreya dāsa
Guru-sevā-devī dāsī
Kaiśorī-devī dāsī
Lalitāmṛta-devī dāsī
Mādhava dāsa
Mādhavendra Puri dāsa
Madhumaṅgala dāsa
Mahāhari dāsa
Nārāyaṇa-kavaca dāsa
Prāṇadā-devī dāsī
Sureśvara dāsa
Varuṇa dāsa
Yamuṇa-devī dāsī

Special thanks to Divya-jñāna dāsa and Nitin Arora for their kind donations to print this book.

Other books by Satsvarūpa dāsa Goswami

Śrīla Prabhupāda

100 Prabhupāda Poems
Beginning at 26 Second Avenue
Calling Out to Śrīla Prabhupāda / Poems and Prayers
He Lives Forever
Here is Śrīla Prabhupāda
Letters from Śrīla Prabhupāda (Vols 1–3)
Life with the Perfect Master
Prabhupāda Appreciation
Prabhupāda-līlā
Prabhupāda Meditations (Vols 1-4)
Prabhupāda Nectar
Remembering Śrīla Prabhupāda
Śrīla Prabhupāda Samādhi Diary

Śāstra/ Essay

A Handbook for Kṛṣṇa Consciousness
Cc. Āśraya
The Daily News: All Things Fail Without Kṛṣṇa
From Copper to Touchstone
Living with the Scriptures
Mukunda Mālā Stotra: The Prayers of King Kulaśekhara
Niti-śāstra: Sayings of Cāṇakya and Hitopadeśa as Quoted By Śrīla Prabhupāda
Qualities of Śrī Kṛṣṇa
Readings in Vedic Literature
Spiritualized Dictionary

Devotional Practices

Begging for the Nectar of the Holy Name
Entering the Life of Prayer
From Imperfection, Purity Will Come About
Japa Reform Notebook (English/ Spanish)
Japa Walks, Japa Talks
Obstacles on the Path of Devotional Service
Reading Reform
Truthfulness, The Last Leg of Religion
Vaiṣṇava Behavior/ 26 Qualities of a Devotee
Vandanaṁ: Handbook of Prayer

Personal Writings

A Poor Man Read's the Bhāgavatam (Vols. 1–3)
A Visit to Jagannātha Purī
Churning the Milk Ocean
Dear Sky: Letters From a Sannyāsī
Every Day, Just Write (Vols. 1–5)
ISKCON in the 1970s: Diaries
Iṣṭa-goṣṭī: Topics for Vaiṣṇava Discussion (Vols. 1–3)
Journal & Poems (Vols. 1-3)
Lessons from the Road (1987–88) (17 volumes)
Memories
Memory in the Service of Kṛṣṇa
My Relationship with Lord Kṛṣṇa
My Search Through Books
Radio Shows
Shack Notes
Passing Places, Eternal Truths
Photo Preaching
The Wild Garden: Collected Writings 1990–1993

Poetry

Dust of Vṛndāvana
Gentle Power
In Praise of the Mahājanas and Other Poems (1983)
Pictures from Bhagavad-gītā As It Is and Other Poems
Prose-poetry at Castlegregory, Ireland
Talking Freely to My Lords
Under the Banyan Tree
The Voices of Surrender and Other Poems
The Waves at Jagannātha Purī
The Worshipable Deity and Other Poems (1984)
Writing in Gratitude

Fiction

Am I A Demon or A Vaiṣṇava?
Choṭa's Way
Gurudeva and Nimāi: Struggling for Survival
Nimāi dāsa and the Mouse: A Fable
Nimāi's Detour: A Story
Śrī Caitanya-Dayā: The Diaries of Harideva and Chayādevī
Viṣṇu-rāta Vijaya: The Story of an Ex-hunter

GN Press Distribution Centers

North America:
PO Box 323
Mifflin, PA 17058
USA
Tel.: 717-436-8232
Fax: 717-436-6432
Email: gnpress@acsworld.net

Europe:
Gaura Bhavan
Cranareen, Kiltegan
Co. Wicklow
Republic of Ireland
Tel.: 353-508-73229

Asia:
C/o Janta Book Depot
23 Shaheed Bhagat Singh Marg
New Delhi 110001
India
Tel.: 91-11-3363685